By Searching

MY JOURNEY THROUGH DOUBT INTO FAITH

ISOBEL KUHN

EDITED BY M. E. TEWKSBURY

OMF BOOKS

Copyright © 2010, OMF International

Published by OMF International
10 West Dry Creek Circle, Littleton CO 80120

ISBN : 978-1-929122-09-7

First published *1959*
This printing *2010*

OMF BOOKS

OMF Books are distributed worldwide.
Visit *www.OMFBooks.com* for more information.

By Searching

ISOBEL KUHN

THE QUESTION THAT PIERCED THE MIST
Canst thou *by searching* find out God?
Job 11:7

THE ANSWER
Ye shall *seek* me, and *find* me, when ye shall search for
me with all your heart.
Jeremiah 29:13

Jesus saith unto him, *I am the way*, the truth, and the
life; no man cometh unto the Father, but by me.
John 14:6

Search the Scriptures . . . they are they
which testify of me.
John 5:39

If any man will do his will, he shall know of the
doctrine, whether it be of God.
John 7:17

CONTENTS

CHAPTER ONE

ON TO THE MISTY FLATS

To every man there openeth
A way, and ways, and a way.
And the high soul climbs the high way,
And the low soul gropes the low.
And in between on the misty flats
The rest drift to and fro.
But to every man there openeth
A high way and a low —
And every man decideth the way his soul shall go
JOHN OKENHAM

"Of course no one in this enlightened age believes any more in the myths of Genesis and —" But here Dr. Sedgewick paused in his lecture as if a second thought had occurred. With a twinkle in his eye, he said, "Well, maybe I had better test it out, before being so dogmatic." Facing the large freshman class, who were hanging on his words, and pulling his face into gravity, he asked: "Is there anyone here who believes there is a heaven and a hell? Who believes that the story of Genesis is true? Please raise your hand." He waited for a response.

Up went my hand as bravely as I could muster courage. I also looked around to see if I had a comrade in my stand. Only one other hand was up, in all that big group of perhaps a hundred students. Dr. Sedgewick smiled. Then, as if sympathetic with our embarrassment, he conceded: "Oh, you just believe that because your papa and mama told you so." He then proceeded with his lecture, assuming once and for all that no thinking human being believed the Bible any more.

Brought up in an earnest Presbyterian home (my grandfather was a Presbyterian minister and my father an ardent lay preacher) I had been carefully coached in the refutations of modernism before my parents had allowed me to enter the university. If it had been a case of arguing the claims of modernism versus fundamentalism, I do not think I would have been shattered in my faith. But there was no argument. There was just the pitying sneer, "Oh, you just believe that because your papa and your mama told you so," and then the confident assumption that no persons nowadays who thought for themselves, who were scientific in their approach to life, believed that old story any more.

On the way home from class I faced the charge honestly. Why did I believe the Bible? The Genesis explanation of life's origin? Why did I believe in heaven and hell?

It was because I had been taught it by my parents and church from the hour I could understand anything. Was that reason enough for accepting it? No. I agreed with Dr. Sedgewick that it was not a sufficient basis to build my life upon. We had experienced remarkable answers to prayer in our family life — didn't that prove the existence of God? But my psychology course taught that mind had a powerful effect over matter. If I had not been so gullible, maybe I could have seen a natural explanation. Our twentieth century believed only when there was a test and a proof. We were scientific in our investigations; we did not swallow the superstitions of our ancestors just because they were handed to us.

Dr. Sedgewick, Professor of the English Department in our university, was an ardent follower of Matthew Arnold's "sweetness and light" philosophy and of Thomas Hardy's materialism. Yet he was so apparently patient and kind toward us whom he felt were still bound by our parents' old-fashioned thinking that he won our affection and respect.

At the end of my walk home I came to the conclusion that I would henceforth accept no theories of life which I had not proved personally. And, quite ignorant of where that attitude would lead me, I had unconsciously stepped off the High Way where man walks with his face lifted Godward and the pure, piney scents of the Heights call him upward. I had stepped on to The Misty Flats, the in-between, level place of easy going — nothing very good attempted, yet nothing bad either. There people walk in the mist, telling each other that no one can see these things clearly. There the in-betweeners drift to and fro. Life has no end but amusement, and no purpose. The herd drifts with the strongest pull and there is no reason for opposing anything. Therefore, they have a kind of peace and a mutual link which they call tolerance.

I did not know that I had stepped down to The Misty Flats. I was just conscious of a sudden pleasant freedom from old duties. If there was no God, why bother to go to church on Sunday, for instance? Why not use Sunday to catch up on sleep, so that I could dance half the night away several times during the week?

Again, if the Bible was but a record of myths and old-fashioned ideas, why read it every morning? That took time. It was much easier to sleep until the very last moment, getting up just in time for the first class at college. Prayer, too, became silly — talking to someone

9

who maybe did not exist.

I would not call myself an atheist because, well, there were those childhood answers to prayer still to be accounted for. But I called myself an agnostic. I frankly did not know if there was a God or not. It was a popular thing to be on The Misty Flats. You had plenty of company. And one was respected as being modern and intelligent to question the old faiths. Life drifted along so pleasantly — for a while.

My home training still had an effect upon me. Jesus Christ, now blurred in the mists which denied His Godhead, was an acknowledged historical character. And His name was still an ointment poured forth to me. He was like a perfume which haunts and calls so that one stops, lifts one's head and drinks it in wistfully. His name was the sweetest melody I knew, and it never failed to stir my heart even though I had ceased to seek Him. His purity and holiness made me hate besmirching things.

All this, because my father and my mother had taught me so.

So when I broke with the old religious habits and frankly went into the world, I was still choosy in what I did. I never smoked. The tainted breath and stained fingers or teeth of the smoker revolted me. I told myself I was too dainty for such doings.

Neither did I drink. My father, brokenhearted at my callous turning of the back on all my home training, still warned me as a medical man what drink could to a girl. "Drink affects men and women biologically, and under its influence girls can be led into sin that they could never consent to when in possession of their senses. Dr. Hall and I have such come to us for consultation all the time. They never meant to, but there they are. Keep away from liquor and you can keep yourself pure, perhaps."

So I did not drink. Also, I had *signed the pledge* when twelve years old, and a certain whimsical loyalty to my childhood self kept me from breaking it.

Amidst the group at the university I was considered *a good girl*, and even a Christian! But I myself knew that I wasn't.

In my studies, I took the honors course in English Language and Literature. It brought me much under the influence of Dr. Sedgewick. But in my extracurricular activities I was mostly interested in the Players Club, the amateur theatrical club of the university. Apparently I had a gift for acting comedy parts, and in my freshman year I won life membership in the Players Club, an honor not usually attained by a first-year student.

The staff patron of our theatricals was Professor H. G. C. Wood, also a member of the English faculty. He was a believer in God and Christ, not an atheist like Dr. Sedgewick. His friendship helped keep me from extremes.

The theater was his hobby and soon became mine. Urgently my mother pleaded with me to attend the Young Women's Christian Association. I went several times, but was frankly bored, so dropped it. I loved the theater, and I liked to dance, and these activities occupied my spare time. In fact, our Varsity 1922 yearbook has, as comment opposite my picture: "And oh the tilt of her heels when she dances!" No shadow of the missionary there.

In my second year I was elected to be secretary of the student council. At that time it was the highest position to which a woman student could be elected. I met the leading young people of the university and became secretly engaged to Ben, one of the star rugby and basketball players.

Ben was a returned soldier from World War I, several years older that I, not handsome, but six feet two or three in height. He came of a good Baptist family and my mother encouraged our friendship. He even took me to his church on Sunday nights! It made a nice inexpensive date, for Ben did not have much money. When he asked me to marry him, he said that our engagement must be kept secret lest his "old man" be angry with him for getting involved before he graduated. I insisted that my parents be told, but his never were. We went together for nearly two years, and my path was perceptibly a downgrade.

CHAPTER TWO

SLIPPERY WAYS IN DARKNESS

*Wherefore their way shall be unto them as slippery ways
in the darkness. They shall be driven on and fall therein,
for I will bring evil upon them,
even the year of their visitation, saith the Lord.*
JEREMIAH 23:12

After experiencing the stretched muscles of climbing, to find oneself on the level is relaxing and pleasant. Therefore The Misty Flats are attractive to foot, eye, and palate *at the beginning*. There is no hint that the pretty mist will gradually close in and bring darkness. There is no suggestion amid the gay chatter of the populous throng that there are slippery places which are going to bring hurt. In the boasted freedom of drifting whither you will, there is certainly no sign that one is being *driven on*, as Jeremiah so shrewdly perceived was the reality. And above all, there is never a hint that the end of The Flats is the visitation of the Lord and the judgment of sin. Yet all that is the real truth.

In my senior year, there came a day when my college chum, Cora, shook me to the foundations with a sentence or so. "Isobel," she said, "I think I should tell you something even though it may hurt. Everybody but you knows that Ben is not loyal to you. He is taking Reba out behind your back."

I turned a stunned face upon her, and her eyes filled with tears of sympathy. With true friendship she went on: "You remember when you were ill and could not go to his fraternity dance?"

"Yes," I replied, "he took Reba in my place that night. He asked me if I would mind, and I said no."

"Well, that was the beginning of it, I guess. They've been seen together a lot. People are talking and I can't bear that you should not know. I don't think he's worth breaking your heart over, Isobel," she said earnestly.

But it did break my heart. It was difficult to believe, and yet I knew he had not been so attentive of late. My father had spoken to me about it. "You have let Ben get too sure of you, Baby," he had said, using his tender pet name for me, the youngest in the family. "Show a man all the love you have *after you are married*, but keep in reserve while you are just engaged. The elemental male *likes* to fight for a mate. What is the use of chasing a streetcar after you've caught it?"

So it was not all Ben's fault. I had been inexperienced — I was still only in my teens. With the promise to be his wife, I had truly given my heart to Ben. Love struggled hard with "maybe if I . . ." and "perhaps I could still win him back." But it was Ben himself who made it hopeless.

I met him one morning at the entrance of the university. No one else was around, so I charged him with taking Reba out behind my back. I wanted to hear from his own lips that it was true, for love rebelled at believing it. He drew himself up to the full stature of his six feet two inches, and I never forget the curl of his lip as he said, "Isobel, you're a softy. You don't suppose, do you, that after we are married, I'm not going to take other women out sometimes?"

"Then we part," I had whispered hoarsely, dazed as if stricken. I was on my way home from a class and have never forgotten the dull agony of that walk. I knew I could never marry a man with such standards of The Misty Flats. I had known the Christ, and I could not be satisfied with less than the ideals He had set before me.

I found myself in the slippery places of darkness. Pride wounded me, love wounded me, and sleep departed from me. The English course I was taking entailed more work than a passing amount. I needed rest during sleep hours, but could not sleep.

My mother was distressed that I should break with Ben and kept saying, "If you would only take my advice." But I could not bear to discuss it with anyone. I discussed it with myself night and day.

My father was my great comfort. He knew enough to be silent and just love me. He even sensed that I was not sleeping. One night when all the house had been asleep for hours and I was still tossing, I heard him come softly into my room. He knelt down beside my bed and prayed God to help me. It only irritated me. "Thanks, Dad," I said wearily. "I know you mean well, but praying doesn't go beyond the ceiling, you know." I never forgot the groan with which he turned away from my agnosticism, and left the room.

The climax came just before Christmas. My birthday is December 17, and I was to be twenty years old, but I do not remember if it was before or after that date. The post office clock on Main Street had just struck two, and I was still tense and tossing. I was desperate. I knew I'd be ill in the morning if I did not get to sleep. Then came the Tempter.

"Of what use is life?" he whispered. "Ben is only an average fellow. Probably all men are just like him.

You'll never find anyone to love you like you want to be loved. Your ideal is too high. And you'd never be happy with a lower ideal of marriage. Why go on with life? It has no purpose, only suffering. This would be a good time to slip out. There is that bottle in the bathroom marked poison. A good long drink and your troubles are over." A good idea. The only sensible solution.

I jumped out of bed and started for the bathroom. *Slippery ways in the darkness: they shall be driven on and fall therein.*

My hand was on the door knob when a deep groan, twice repeated, broke the silence of the dark. It was my father, moaning in his sleep in the next room. I was not afraid, for I recognized Father's tones, but I was startled into remembrance of him. I stood with my hand on the knob debating. If I committed suicide, Daddy would think I had gone to hell. Of course that would not make a place called hell, but how terrible for Daddy to think so. He had been such a dear, kind father to me all my life. Dare I make him such a dastardly return? No, I couldn't be so mean and selfish.

In agony I turned, sat down on the edge of my bed and faced the darkest moment of my life. I didn't want to live, and I couldn't die! Oh the black despair of The Misty Flats! How little did I know of the golden sunshine pouring on the High Way above them! What a lot of heartache I might have been saved if I had only been told that God had already laid His hand on a man who was to be a dear husband to me with the same ideals and the same passion for God's highest purposes! But first I had to drink to the dregs the emptiness of the promises held out by The Misty Flats. Only then could I be freed from their lure and subtle call.

Now a strange thing happened. That day I had been studying Matthew Arnold's essay on *The Study of Poetry*. (You remember, it was Sedgewick, a disciple of

Arnold, who had first pushed me off the High Way?) In that essay he gives various quotations from the classics as touchstones of perfect poetry. One such was from Dante and ran: *In la sua volontade e nostra pace.* From my knowledge of Latin I had guessed the meaning: *In His will is our peace.* Now that sentence wrote itself across the dark of my bedroom. Dante believed in God. What if there was a God, after all? If so, I certainly had not been in His will. Maybe that was why I had no peace. An idea struck me. No one was watching to see if I were a fool or not. Sitting there on my bed's edge, I raised both hands heavenward. "God, if there be a God," I whispered, for I was not going to believe in what did not exist just to get a mental opiate, "if You will prove to me that You are, and if You will give me peace, I will give You my whole life. I'll do anything You ask me to do, go where You send me, obey You all my days." Then I climbed into bed and pulled the blankets over me.

CHAPTER THREE

WHAT YOU SHOULD NOT IMITATE

The next thing I knew, it was morning. The golden sunshine of a December day in Vancouver poured into my bedroom. I lay there drowsily enjoying it when a thought suddenly startled me into full consciousness. I had been sleeping like a baby — how had it happened?

Memory traced itself back to the experience of the night before. I had made a bargain with God. I had asked Him for peace, and — peace had come. Oh yes, answered Reason, but that was easily explainable apart from God. That was no proof that God existed. It was just the effect of mind over matter. I had committed my troubles to an imaginary being and that was why body and mind quieted down.

Restlessly I threw off the bedclothes and sat on the edge of my bed. I was not going to use religion as an opiate. I was going to be realistic or nothing. As a matter of fact, I believe I was born with "a flair for reality." But as I pondered, the thought persisted: "You made a bargain last night. The Other Side kept His part. There was no stipulation as to how peace should come, *and it came*. Nobody knows about it and nobody will know, if this should prove to be foolishness. Why not continue your part of the agreement and see?"

But what was my part? To yield my whole life if He

proved Himself. And in the meantime, why not try to seek Him?

Seek God? Where?

Can a man by searching find out God? Zophar had questioned Job, obviously not believing it possible. Job had tried to answer by pointing to God in His creative works. But the twentieth century had another theory for the origin of the earth.

Where does one go to search for God? Even as I asked myself that question, a picture from memory floated before me. It was at the Guelph conference of 1921 when the Student Christian Movement was formed. A young man was on his feet giving his testimony. "While I was interned in Germany as a prisoner of war," he said, "I got hold of a Bible and started to read it. I found God through reading His Word."

I had been a university delegate for the YWCA to that convention, but had apparently been unaffected by it. I knew there was a conflict between the modernist students and the fundamentalists. This young ex-soldier was earnest for the old beliefs. I was still an agnostic and weary of religious arguments. I let them talk and did not let it enter my heart. But this young fellow was aglow with something real. He was the outstanding memory of that conference to me, yet I did not even know his name.

Now in my own hour of need I could see him standing there, radiant, affirming he had *found God*. And he had found Him through the Christ of the New Testament.

Well, I had a Bible. There it was on my bookshelf, unused, a bit dusty, but beautiful and new — a gift from my father when I graduated from high school. I pulled it down and looked at it.

Modernists said the Pentateuch was not written by Moses. This was questioned, that was questioned. Was there anything that wasn't questioned? Yes — the historicity of Jesus Christ is beyond doubt. And the four Gospels are accepted as a more or less authentic record of His teachings, as authoritative as Plato's were of Socrates, at least.

So I decided to search for God through Jesus Christ, to read the Gospels only, to underline everything and anything that Jesus said *to do* and try honestly to do them. Jesus prayed, so I would begin to try praying again — cautiously, of course, and not really assuming that it went any higher than the ceiling. With that decided, I arose and dressed for another day's study at the University of British Colombia.

Now began a life at two levels: an outer level of study, worldly gaiety, and pride, and an inner level of watching, seeking after God — if there was a God. Always I added that.

God is not a puppet. Man may not pull strings and expect Him to perform — not even doctrinally correct strings, such as Balaam tried to pull. God is not man's servant that a puny atheist may shout a challenge and He is bound to respond. Neither is God a genie, that if man is lucky enough to find the right combination of words, He will suddenly pop out and reveal Himself. God is our Creator, all powerful and dwelling in light unapproachable. He demands reverence. But He is also willing to be Father to such as come to Him by His ordained road, Jesus Christ. As Father He tenderly stoops to the immaturity of the babe in Christ.

This is the only explanation I have to offer for the following facts. God answered prayers which were unworthy even to have been brought before His presence. If I prayed those same prayers today He would *not* answer them. He responded then, ignoring the selfish vanity of the request, simply because of the honest seeking at the base. He knew I meant it when I said I would give Him my whole life. *The Father seeketh such to worship Him — in spirit and in truth.*

For some three months after my "bargain" I experienced nothing convincing. I read the Gospels and prayed in private, but did not go to church or show any outward interest in religion. Then one day I was invited to a private dance at the home of a girl friend, Jill. Jill had moved away to a different part of town and probably did not know that I had broken with Ben. As she did not inquire as to whether or not I wanted him as my partner, I had no opportunity to tell her. She usually gave a dance once a season and invited Ben only because he went with me, her friend. She usually just invited him and left it to him to arrange for my escort to and from her house. So as I prepared to go, I wondered if he would be there.

On my arrival he wasn't there, and I prepared to enjoy the evening thoroughly. It was a small home dance with just our crowd, and I loved my friends dearly. Jill's new house was center-halled, so that for dancing we had three spaces: parlor, hall, and dining room. I was dancing with Les, Cora's friend, and long since her dear husband, when it happened. We had circled out into the hall when the doorbell rang. Jill opened the door and I saw Ben, Reba with him, and he was ushering her into the house! I could hardly believe that he would have dared to do such a thing. It was like slapping my face publicly. And the dance was so small that there was no avoiding constant contact. I became completely unnerved. Trembling from head to foot, I began to walk all over Les's feet. Long hours of study, late hours of dancing, unhappy broken sleep had wrecked my nerves. I was undone — there was simply no escape from the humiliating fact. Les's look of respectful compassion did not help my chagrin. I could not fool Les about the cause of my agony, and the knowledge was too much for my pride.

"Les, I don't feel well — will you please excuse me?" I said. Stopping at the foot of the hall staircase, I fled up to the bedroom assigned as our dressing room. Up and down the floor I paced in a rage at myself, trying to use pride to whip my trembling body into control. It was perfectly useless; I shook like an aspen leaf.

Suddenly I remembered I was trying to prove if there was a God. With almost a sneer at such a ridiculous thing, I nevertheless prayed, "O God, if you are, please give me p—" but I did not have time to finish the sentence. Something like an electric current struck me, shot me through; and I tingled all over. It had come from above and from outside myself.

It left me completely poised and quiet. Incredulous, I stretched out my hand. It was steady and firm. Without stopping to say, "Thank You," and marveling inwardly, I turned and ran down the stairs. That same dance number was still on, and Les was still standing at the foot of the staircase where I had left him.

"I'm all right now, Les," I said gaily. "Let's finish." Which we did.

A wonderful exultation, a feeling as if I had new life, pulsed through me and continued all evening. Ben asked for a dance and made no effort to conceal his admiration. "You are beautiful tonight," he whispered, but I gave an evasive answer. Our ideals were too different. I could not let my affections get involved again.

The evening was a triumph of gratified pride and vanity for me. But when I was alone in my bedroom, emotional reaction set in. Ben was a superb dancer, and my longing to float through life in perfect rhythm together with him would not be challenged by common sense. Sleep again departed from me, and I tossed in agony until morning.

One fact stood out. I had cried to God for help. My

lips twisted in sardonic unbelief that He even existed, but He had answered swiftly. This was no case of mind acting upon matter, for my mind had held no faith at all. But help had come *from the outside entirely*. I was now convinced that some Force outside me, intelligent, loving, and powerful, was up there trying to get in touch with me. Never again did I pray *if Thou art*.

Now I wanted to know — how much could I ask of Him? Did He always answer prayer in Jesus' name? Morning and night I now prayed in faith. Those prayers were still all selfish, and this is the part of my story where I do not want any young readers to try to imitate me.

Follow me in my pursuit of God, yes. Like me, come to Him by way of the Christ of Calvary, yes. Seek for the revelation of that Christ in the Bible, yes. But don't imitate my flounderings. I was pigheaded now in the matter of refusing all human advice, and my own level of living was so low that God could not meet me on a higher one.

I wondered if God could answer seemingly impossible requests. For instance, would He get me invitations to certain balls and dances? It was our senior year and almost all of our "gang" were paired off now, either engaged or going steady. There was no one within the circle of my close acquaintances who would be free to invite me unless I hinted, which I did not intend to do, ever. God answered prayer wonderfully, causing my incredulity to marvel at *His power* to do it. I will tell of one instance.

A neighboring university had sent their football teams to play ours, and a *thé dansant* was to be given to the two teams after the match. It was purposely a small affair in honor of the teams, just the players and their girl friends and such team officers as the coach and manager. Ben was one of the star players, and I wanted to go. He had barged in on my party; now I wanted to go to this affair held in his honor to show that I was not dependent on him for a good time. Not only was I moved by a thoroughly low and fleshly reason, but also it was hopeless to expect an invitation to such an exclusive party. Could God do it? I challenged Him.

At last the day before the match arrived. No one would ask me now. It would be an insult for any man to ask a girl at such a late hour, sure proof that she was only second or third choice.

That last afternoon a fellow student and I had arranged a rehearsal of a theatrical scene in which he and I were to act alone. George was a good friend of mine and engaged to a girl called Martha. He also happened to be on the manager's staff of the football team, but this I did not know then. He had come to my house for the rehearsal, and after it was over and he reached for his hat to leave, he said, "Well Isobel, see you at the *thé dansant* tomorrow afternoon after the match." Then I saw that he did not know I had broken with Ben.

"No, I don't think you will, George," I said slowly.

He whirled around and shot me a keen look. Then, gentleman that he was, he drew himself up and said with fine courtesy, "Isobel, last night Martha was called out of town unexpectedly. I thought I was going to have to 'go stag' to the *thé dansant*. May I have the pleasure of your company? I'll explain to Martha — I'm sure she won't mind."

It was just as simple as that. I was almost intoxicated with the wonder of it, and again the afternoon was a great triumph for me. I had more partners seeking me than there were dances, while Reba was more than once a wallflower. In fact, while dancing with me, Ben had to excuse himself to go and find her a partner!

Now, do I really believe God was responsible for that? I am sure God gave it to me. Moreover, by piling on the triumphs He taught me a lesson I never forgot. I learned that pride and gratified vanity could never bring me peace or happiness. Underneath the gay triumphant surface I was miserable. My heart was often like lead, even while my lips were chattering merry nonsense. This kind of life would never satisfy me. I grew more and more unhappy and disillusioned. And that was what God wanted. It was as if He said, "If this is what you think you want, dear, have some more!" And He stuffed the froth of life down me. Yet every time He got me an invitation when humanly speaking it seemed impossible, He proved to me again that there was nothing He could not do for me.

All during this time, my parents knew nothing of my inward seekings. They sensed a change going on, but I still refused to go to church with them and usually spent Sunday trying to catch up on the sleep I had lost at dances during the week! But there may have been a softening visible, for Mother began again to try to help me.

"Isobel, I want you to come with me to hear Professor Ellis. The meeting is just a Bible class, not held in a church, but in a classroom of the Vancouver Bible School. Just to please your mother. Won't you do a little thing like this to please me? I don't want to go alone."

So I went.

I did not know that anyone else in that room knew me. In fact, I did not look at the audience, for I had ceased to be interested in human beings. But the speaker held my attention. Professor Ellis was a cultured, educated Christian gentleman. I liked his quiet, refined manner of speech. He was speaking that day on the temptation of Christ, and as he went on to give his message, he also very frankly pointed out the liberal interpretation of that passage. Without any belligerent dogmatism, he courteously but deftly refuted their arguments. I saw clearly that here was a scholar who knew both sides of the argument. Here was a real gentleman who would never stoop to nasty remarks about an opponent. Watching the quiet radiance of his face, I instinctively knew that here was a man who had *personal experience with God*. I decided that this was the preacher for me. I would come again.

Seated behind me was another Christian gentleman. White headed, shy, and reserved, he was known to me only as Mr. Wright, a friend of my father's. I forget if it was the first time I went to Professor Ellis' Bible class, or on a succeeding occasion, but at the close of the meeting he leaned forward and spoke to me.

"Isobel, I'm glad to see you here," he said, his eyes flooded with tears. "I've been praying for you for some seven years."

I was stunned. It was about seven years since I had decided to dance and go in for worldly things against my father's pleadings. The yearning in Christ which lit up Mr. Wright's face stirred me to the depths, for my soul still knew periods of agony. With eyes as flooded as his own, I tried to murmur, "Thank you," then escaped quickly from the building.

But every Sunday saw me back in that afternoon service, and weekly I was fed and nourished in the truth of God's Word. Professor Ellis' scholarship and his expository preaching combined with his gentle culture had won my full confidence, and I was willing to learn from him.

Though my head was still befogged by the mists of The Flats, my feet were once more planted on the High Way, prepared to climb. My face was steadfastly turned Godward.

CHAPTER FOUR
MY YEAR IN ARABIA

On graduating in May 1922 at twenty years of age, I needed only five months of Normal School to qualify for a teacher's certificate. My ambition was to be a dean of women and teach English in some university. But I was so young and inexperienced in teaching that I first had to accept an elementary grade school assignment.

I could have taken an up-country high school appointment, but Mother would not hear of it. She insisted that I teach in a city school. Because of my inexperience I had to accept a position as teacher of the third grade at the Cecil Rhodes School, Vancouver.

In the meantime, my family had moved. My father was roentgenologist to Dr. Ernest Hall of Victoria, B.C. Mother sold our Vancouver home and purchased a chicken ranch just outside Victoria. This ranch was to be for my brother who had been a soldier in World War I and for whom employment must be found. He thought he would like ranch life.

So in February 1923 I found myself a "schoolmarm" in Vancouver and needing to find a boardinghouse. For the first time in my life I would not live at home, but would be on my own, receiving a monthly salary for which I need account to no one. The idea was distinctly pleasing. But where would I board?

Somehow I ran into the mother of a girl with whom I had gone to elementary school eight years before. They were a Scottish family, and the mother especially was a very superior person. Mrs. McMillan was a thinker, but, inbred with theosophy, had fallen in with the idea that it was wrong to spank a child. I have wondered if this wasn't the reason her children did more as they liked than as she liked. The two youngest would not continue school, so had to take employment below their family cultural level. By the time I graduated, Mrs. McMillan was so reduced in circumstances that she was trying to run a boardinghouse.

She asked if I would come to her. She was apologetic, for she had lost her best furniture and could not provide anything as comfortable as I had been accustomed to, but she was very clean, an excellent cook, and her house was within walking distance of my school. Mother knew her and felt at ease that I should be with Mrs. McMillan, who was as loving and kind to me as if I were her own child.

So I found myself in this house, the only Christian. The two daughters were both engaged to sailors. The youngest child, a son, was a policeman with a wife and small baby. The policeman's brother-in-law, whom we called Laurie, attended Normal School, hoping to become a schoolteacher. As he was not yet earning, he paid a minimum rate of board, if anything. This was the household among whom I became the ninth.

After graduation my particular clique scattered. Many went to other universities for further degrees. Some taught school, but went upcountry where they could get high school positions. In no time at all I seemed alone and living in a different world.

The young people of my boardinghouse were very nice to me, but were all for life's pleasures. I did not care to join them. We had little in common but our boardinghouse. Surrounded with young laughter and noise, I was as alone as if I had been in the deserts of Arabia. For a year and a half God shut me up to that aloneness, so that I have always called it *my year in Arabia*.

A young fellow we will call Mac had begun to ask me out. He was still studying and invited me to the various big dances of the university from time to time, but as he did not live in Vancouver, our dates were not frequent.

I had begun to attend evening lectures at the Vancouver Bible School, but it was just beginning and I do not remember meeting other Christian young people. I was lonely.

F. B. Meyer in *Abraham* points out that this is one of the planned training schools of God. "One symptom of being on that path is loneliness." He continues:

Nothing strengthens us so much as isolation and transplantation . . . under the wholesome demand his soul will put forth all her native vigor . . . it may not be necessary for us to withdraw from home and friends, but we shall have to withdraw our heart's deepest dependence from all earthly props and supports if ever we are to learn what it is to trust simply and absolutely on the eternal God.

For one thing, I found it hard to keep my prayer times. The others in the house played cards and danced or had what they called a good time until long past midnight. I could not pray with those noises in my ears. To get up early to pray was not the answer, for once I was up my mind went rushing on to my school teaching, which I was finding difficult.

At last I hit on the plan of asking the Lord to wake

me up at two o'clock in the morning, after the house had settled to quiet when I would arise for an hour's prayer and Bible study. This worked wonders. Always a sleepyhead, it was wonderful to me to be awakened each morning — as I was. And in the quiet of that still hour, Christ became so real to me that often I felt I could have touched Him if I only put out my hand. I was learning what Dr. A. W. Tozer calls "the awareness of His presence." It satisfied me as nothing on earth had ever done and filled me with a joy of communion that is inexpressible. In this Arabia I learned fellowship with Christ, a living Person-to-person fellowship which from then on became dearer than anything else in life to me.

The acute sense of His presence was not given during the first few months I was at the McMillan boardinghouse. My head was still in The Misty Flats, and my feet were too entangled with the world. How I got lifted out into a clear spiritual atmosphere is a story in itself, so I give it here.

It began with an angry disappointment.

I must first explain that I was not happy teaching third grade eight-year-olds. The children in my class fascinated me. It was my first real connection with children, for I was the baby of our family and we had early moved away from where small cousins lived. I was totally inexperienced with children and thought them "the cutest things." Even their little buttons of noses fascinated me. Needless to say, I had discipline problems! The little cherubs soon found out that their teacher was a softy. She was given daily samples of what unexpectedly naughty things a cherub can think up — even without ever losing his angelic smile!

Then the subjects I taught were so elementary: spelling, arithmetic tables, simple nature studies, and physical drill. Eight hours each day, one's delightful mental life must be tied down to such boredom. I have often thought that if I had been allowed to teach high school English I might never have become a missionary. I would have loved it.

But now I hated teaching. I found the discipline so perplexing that I was afraid I was going to be a failure and became thoroughly alarmed. This was to be my life work! I decided I must study teaching and signed up for a Teachers' Convention in Seattle during — was it Easter holidays? I've forgotten.

I had a friend in Seattle who had corresponded with me since grade school, which we had attended together — the General Wolfe School in south Vancouver. I had not seen Donald for years, but when I wrote that I was coming to the convention I got a letter right back saying I must stay at his house. He would be at the boat to meet me. So it was arranged.

I was just about to leave for the Seattle boat when I was handed a telegram. It read: HAVE ARRANGED FOR YOU TO STAY AT WHIPPLES SEATTLE LOVE DADDY.

Was I annoyed! "Daddy, how perfectly mean of you," I muttered to myself. "Oh, when will you and Mother stop interfering with my plans and realize that I am grown up?" The Whipples — who are they? Dim memory finally produced vague outlines. "Oh, religious friends of Dad's. Yes, I remember now. So *that's* Dad's idea. Wants to have them talk to me about my soul, eh? Well, they won't find a porcupine more receptive. I'm just *not* going to be bossed like this. I'll wire them that I've made other plans."

A glance at the clock showed me I had no time to send a telegram if I were to catch the ship. Thoroughly provoked I went aboard to my cabin. By morning we would be in Seattle.

Don was there all right and I explained my predicament. He was not put out. "Well, just sleep there," he suggested. "I can take you around from there." And so it was decided.

I don't remember anything about the convention. I remember a nice supper with Don afterward, and an evening of fun — a dance perhaps. I did not realize how late the hour was until we approached the Whipple house and found it in darkness. No — there was a dim light at the back. The door bell ring produced other lights, then the door was opened by Mrs. Otis Whipple herself. Don was introduced and invited in, but he declined and said good-bye — and I found myself in the sitting room alone with my hostess.

I do not know the kind of person I was looking for, but it certainly was not the kind I met. Motherly plumpness, a cheery voice, southern warmth of hospitality, geniality and culture were what greeted me. Culture is a form of beauty, the beauty of a trained mind and heart, trained to think of the other person's feelings. Beauty of any kind has always had power over me, and I was drawn to her immediately. Instinctively I knew she was not one to barge into my inner sanctum without an invitation. As yet I did not know there are other ways of soul winning!

God and my soul were never mentioned — just a charming talk about my home, their old friendship with my father, of a girl, Tony Black, to whom I was supposed to bear striking likeness. She spoke of a summer conference at a place called The Firs and of her husband's sister, a missionary in China, recently widowed who was to be at The Firs this summer of 1923. More and more I relaxed; better and better I liked her. When I was finally shown to my room, my porcupine quills were all safely laid flat.

The next day was Sunday. I had resolved to bend to decorum enough to go to church in the morning. Then I meant to claim the rest of the day to do what I liked.

34

I had a friend named Mamie in the city and had an appointment to spend the afternoon with her.

I wondered idly at the fact that Mrs. Whipple had not yet made any effort to get me alone and talk religiously. Little did I dream the truth, which she told me only years later. That first night after we had all gone to bed, she could not sleep for the burden of me. At last she got up and fell to her knees, asking God the cause. For more than an hour she battled in prayer that whatever the reason He had sent me to them, it might be fulfilled before I left. Not before she felt she had prayed *through* did she go back to bed. Having committed the matter to the Lord, she did not get anxious as to how He would accomplish it. She did not try to rush matters, which in my case would have been the end of her possibly influencing me. One of her favorite sayings was, "Flexible in the hands of the Spirit." She truly lived it.

The afternoon visit to Mamie was very pleasant (I had always loved her) until she asked me an unsettling question: "Isobel, do you like school teaching? Are you enjoying your work?"

"Oh, Mamie," I groaned in reply, "I'm not happy at all. All my life I've planned to teach, and now that I've graduated and am at it, I feel like a misfit. I just hate it. If only I had a high school position, I'm sure it would be different. I'm still sure I would enjoy teaching literature. But I'm only twenty-one, you know, and so could not expect to get right into a city high school without any teaching experience. It's so inane teaching spelling and arithmetic. I just don't —"

"Isobel, I know what you need," struck in Mamie earnestly. "You need to see a phrenologist and have your head read! He'd tell you what you are fitted for. And it just so happens that a very excellent phrenologist is in town, Dr. X–. He is a friend of ours and coming to supper with us tonight. His charges are very high, but as a friend of ours I'm sure he would do you for nothing. But you would have to come tonight, because he is leaving tomorrow."

"Oh, Mamie!" I cried. "How perfectly wonderful! There is only one snag. I'm staying with religious people, and they might be offended at a guest in their house going to see a phrenologist on Sunday. You know how particular some people are about keeping the Sabbath. Oh, if they will only consent! My hostess is really a dear, and I just couldn't offend her. But I tell you — I'll go right back and ask her. If she says yes, I'll phone you, and you make the appointment for me. Oh, it would be grand to be happy in one's work! It would be wonderful to know what one was fitted for in life."

"Well, Dr. X– will know, I'm sure of that. All right. Goodbye. I'll be looking for that phone call!"

We parted, I to return to the Whipples' home with beating heart. Was I about to lose the opportunity of my life because of old-fashioned religious scruples?

Arriving back earlier than expected, I met Mrs. Whipple in the hall and went straight to the point. "Mrs. Whipple, I would like to ask you a question," I said. "Would you object to my going to a phrenologist tonight to have my head read? I've not been very happy in my work and —"

"Well now, dear," she said in her cheery, comfortable way, "let's go upstairs and discuss it. I'm not quite sure I understand all that is involved. Here is Miss McCausland" — waylaying another guest who was crossing the hall at that moment. "Miss McCausland is a schoolteacher herself, and maybe she can help us. Take her to the little front bedroom, Margaret. I'll be there in a moment."

I did not learn until many years later why she delayed in coming. She ran for prayer help. Her young high school daughter, Lois, was in the back of the house with two friends, all of them in their teens. It is interesting now to look back at those three little maidens who were urged on to their knees downstairs to intercede for the right direction of phrenologist-seeker me upstairs. Lois later became Mrs. Nathan Walton of the China Inland Mission. Evelyn Watson became her sister-in-law, Mrs. Elden Whipple, while the third young girl, Doris Coffin, became Mrs. Willard Aldrich, author of the well-known column in *Moody Monthly*, "Out of the Mixing Bowl." But at this moment the three teenagers were only told, "Isobel has come to a crisis in her life! Pray her through while I go upstairs and deal with her." So down on their knees they went in prayer.

Upstairs, Mrs. Whipple said to me, "Now dear, tell us everything from the beginning so we will understand."

The floodgates were unlocked and out poured the story of my school teaching troubles and disappointments. I spoke freely because I felt an atmosphere of loving sympathy, and sensed a poise about those two women which seemed to say that their lives were satisfying. I unfolded this wonderful opportunity of having my head read by a skilled phrenologist, and the supposed snag — it was Sunday. With beating heart, I looked up into that kind, wise, and lovely face and said, "Would you object to my going on Sunday?"

No tremor of horror or shock crossed her face, but she had a look of deep thoughtfulness as if she were weighing the matter carefully.

Then came her answer: "Isobel, dear, I don't think the matter of its being Sunday is the important thing. It's like this: God has a plan for your life. The Bible says that He has created us unto good works and foreordained that we should walk in them (Eph. 2:10). That means He has foreordained a useful life for you, and

He does so for each of His creatures. The point as I see it is to find out God's plan for your life and then follow it. If it is His will to reveal that plan through a phrenologist, going on Sunday would do no harm. But if it were not His will to reveal His plan through a phrenologist, going any day of the week would be wrong."

I was struck with the common sense and logic of her words and thrilled through and through to hear that God had a plan for my life. Daughter of an elder in the church and granddaughter of a Presbyterian minister, I do not remember anyone ever telling me that before. I had always thought God was a kindly, fatherly Being, away off in the heavens somewhere. We could call upon Him in trouble, but for the rest of the time it was up to us to map out our own lives in good, honest work. Then we could ask His blessing and help from time to time. That God was so minutely interested in me, that He would take the trouble to plan a career for me — plan it without my asking — the tender intimacy of a Love which could do that touched me to the breaking point. Hardly able to control my voice, I asked, "Well, how are we to find out His plan for us?"

By this time I was kneeling at the bed on which Miss McCausland sat, Mrs. Whipple in a chair beside me. She reached for her Bible and opened it in front of me saying, "Isobel, I've always found His will through His Word, this Book. His plan for us will always be in accordance with the Scriptures. And with me, it is usually from the Bible itself that I get my leading." At that moment the telephone rang, and Mrs. Whipple was called.

"Excuse me a moment, I'll be right back," she said. "Miss McCausland, will you tell Isobel what you think?"

I do not remember what dear Miss McCausland said, for I was thinking, *God's plan for my life is in that*

Book. Impulsively, I pulled it toward me. It fell shut, and I reopened it at random with my eyes on Miss McCausland. Inwardly I was wondering what the Bible had to say about phrenology, when my eye happened to fall on the open page and there, unconsciously, my left hand lay with the forefinger pointing at a verse. I read, "Keep thee far from a false matter" (Ex. 23:7).

It was as if a voice had spoken to me. I was so startled at the directness of the answer to my inward question that my distressed heart collapsed with relief. I was weeping when Mrs. Whipple reentered the room — weeping terribly, simply rent with sobs.

"It is all right, Isobel," she tried to say. "He'll lead you."

"Oh, He has," I cried. "Look at this verse!" and pointed to *Keep thee far from a false matter*. She, too, marveled at such a quick, thoroughly complete answer.

The piled-up heartaches of a whole year and half of *searching* after God had reached a climax, and I could only sob until exhausted. Tenderly and lovingly the two ladies ministered to me. Dear Mrs. Whipple never tried to pry; the privacy of the human soul was respected by her, and that was another reason we all loved and trusted her so.

I do not remember anything more of that visit, except that Mrs. Whipple told me again of The Firs Bible Conference and urged me to attend that July as her guest. I was not interested. I still shrank from evangelistic meetings with their worked-up emotion and high pressure methods. I did not intend to be high pressured into anything.

"Thank you, Mrs. Whipple," I said, "but I have already signed up to attend Teachers' Summer School in Victoria. Until God leads differently, I must earn my living and can only do it by teaching." And so we parted.

The Lord now wished to direct my thoughts into a

channel where they would never have run of themselves. My life was about to turn a new corner. Strange to say, it all hinged, at first, upon a pair of shoes. But that is the subject of the next chapter.

CHAPTER FIVE

A PAIR OF SHOES AND
THE FIRS CONFERENCE

"**H**ere, Julia," Mrs. Tom Cole said to her sister-in-law, Mrs. Otis Whipple. "The Firs Conference will soon open, and you need a pair of shoes." With a significant look she held out a five-dollar bill.

I do not know if those were her exact words, but the gift was given for shoes — and a significant look along with it, as Mrs. Cole told me herself, years later.

Julia Whipple was not one to neglect her personal appearance. To be well groomed had been her life-long habit. But of late, funds had not been too plentiful. The story of how Julia and Otis Whipple gave the Lord their last earthly possession — this honeymoon cabin at The Firs, Bellingham, Washington — and of how God used it to establish the annual Lake Whatcom Bible and Missionary Conference has been told by Doris Coffin Aldrich in a book called The Firs of the Lord. Suffice it to say that 1923 was to be only their third attempt at a conference, and Julia Whipple was to be hostess. What would people think of her shabby shoes?

But she had something else on her mind.

She had been praying that Isobel Miller would come to The Firs Conference. She saw, as I had not, that here was one groping blindly toward God and open to dangerous misleadings if she were not carefully grounded in the Word. I might be carried off my feet by some magnetic personality of one of the many "isms," if I chanced to meet one at this stage. I needed grounding in the Scriptures, and I needed Christian fellowship. I had a small college debt to pay and had been earning a salary for only six months. Maybe money would be a factor in bringing me. At any rate, she waved the matter of new shoes aside, sat down, and wrote a letter urging me to come. The enclosed five dollars, she said, was what she felt to be the Lord's provision for my boat tickets. Once I reached The Firs I was to be her guest; room and board would cost me nothing. Wouldn't I come?

I received her gift and invitation quite casually, not at all moved with any desire to go. It was Mrs. Whipple's kind heart, I told myself, and now I was forced to do something about it.

I felt my excuse would be an easy one to make. The conference came right in the middle of the summer school I had signed up for. I must get credit for this summer's study, and they would hardly give me full credit for six weeks' work if I ran off in the middle for ten or eleven days! So I made this my test, and I prayed about it: "Lord, if it be your will for me to go, please move the authorities to grant consent without reducing my credits, and I'll take it as your will I am to go."

The next morning found me before the registrar of the Teachers' Summer Institute. "I have been called to Bellingham on a matter important to me and would like to apply for ten days' absence without reducing my credits. Could that be done, sir?" I asked.

He inquired my name, turned over the pages of a book, pursed his lips a moment, then said, "All right, Miss Miller. Just tell us when you leave and when you will return."

I could not believe my ears. On the day before, a fellow student teacher had applied for a week off and had been flatly refused! I still do not know how to explain it, but my full credits were given to me.

I came out of the office walking as if in a dream. I inquired about the boat schedule and sent word to Mrs. Whipple that I was coming, how and when, and went home to pack my suitcase.

So it came about that one evening in July, 1923, my boat arrived at the Bellingham pier. I had never been there before and knew no one. As I looked eagerly around for Mrs. Whipple, a young man and a sweet-faced girl stepped up to me.

"Isobel Miller? We've come to meet you. Elden Whipple and Evelyn Watson — do you remember meeting us in Seattle? We have a car here. Hop in! We have to drive to the conference grounds, but it is not too far."

Their warm friendliness made me feel at home immediately and soon we were whirling out over curving roads with fragrant woods on either hand. It was a twisting labyrinth to me, but finally we turned into a path, drew up among tall fir trees, and there was dear Mrs. Whipple coming to meet me. Her radiance, rippling laugh of joy, and overflowing hospitality was something to cuddle down into. I was duly hugged and kissed, then shown into a big firelit room.

Older people sat on chairs and the younger ones on the floor before the big, crackling open fireplace of logs. The flames threw a golden light over all faces. The young people pulled me down on the floor to sit with them while the evening devotional service continued. Though always shy and reticent with strangers, here I was soon at home and filled with a wonderful content. The atmosphere was charged with the presence of the One I was learning to know and adore. He was the center of everyone else's attention too.

In the doorway, I had been introduced to "my sister-in-law, Mrs. Edna Whipple Gish, whose story I told you in Seattle. She is to be your cabin mate." Years afterward I asked Mrs. Whipple if this had been a premeditated arrangement, for it was to have a lasting effect on my life.

"I can't remember that it was," she said simply. "Edna's was the only cabin with a spare space, as I remember it."

After the campfire service, Edna led me through a woodsy path to the little cabin in the woods where she and I were to live. We slept together, but before going to sleep she pulled out a little worn Bible from beneath her pillow and read a chapter with me. She prayed. Then at "lights out" we settled down with the perfume of the fir trees soothing us into slumber.

I had time to think back over Edna's story just before falling asleep.

"This is Ellis's Bible," she had said to me as she reverently took the worn, much-marked book from beneath the pillow. Then I remembered what Mrs. Whipple had told me in Seattle.

Edna had met Ellis when he was on his first furlough and found him her ideal. He was a young man of deep devotion and consecration. Together they had gone to China to the South Gate section of Nanking.

The next year they went for their vacation to beautiful Kuling, a famous mountain resort where there is a pool and good swimming and also many lovely walks.

One morning they had decided on a swim. Both were expert swimmers. As they left their tent, they heard a cry from the pool. Ellis immediately ran and dived in to the rescue. A young missionary had caught a cramp and gone down. Ellis was successful and saved her life, but he himself disappeared. Edna dived in to search for him. As time dragged on and she could not find him, one can imagine the terror and anguish of her feelings. Diving, searching, she did not notice that her body was being bruised and battered against the rocks. Ellis — that was all she thought of. Finally she saw his body washed up behind a little waterfall. Again she dived, reached him, dragged his body with her and got it to shore. But life was gone.

Exhausted, she sank on a tree stump and covered her face with her hands.

A few minutes later she happened to look up and saw some Chinese coolies standing terrified with the dead man before them. Quickly she approached them and explained that the body on the ground was not her husband — he was safe with God — and she preached Christ to them.

Edna was so bruised that she was sent to the hospital and later advised to take a short furlough. Ellis's insurance money was enough to bring her to The Firs for the summer, and the conference council asked her to lead the young people's meetings.

We never knew what it cost her to set aside her daily heartbreak and be our cheery, radiant Bible teacher. Years later Mrs. Whipple told me how Edna would go to the council and tell them she could not continue, but they would promise to pray for her, and back she would come to us.

She laid before us the scriptural challenge to a consecrated life and to missionary service. I had never given the foreign field one thought up to that time. I was a stay-at-home body by disposition and a veritable slave to physical comforts. Travel never attracted me; it meant strange faces and strange words — in other words, discomfort. Edna was the first to show me that I ought to be willing to give this up if God asked me to do so.

When she finally gave a challenge to those who would surrender for foreign service if He called, I put up my hand. I was surprised to see how thrilled she was. To me it was a matter of course. That night I had made my bargain with God; I had promised Him my life. If He wanted it on the foreign field, why, of course, I must go to the foreign field. It was not a question of if I wanted to go or not — I was no longer my own. At the time I had no clear indication that it was the foreign field He wanted. I was willing, if it were, to go — that was all. Why were they all so excited that I had raised my hand?

Edna had unwittingly brought a much deeper blessing. Cabin life with her was my first encounter with a Spirit-filled life living its daily routine habits. It was Edna off the platform who wrought most for me.

She sought the Lord's face before that of anyone else at the beginning of each day. There was no wake-up chatter and pillow-flinging nonsense at dawn. This deeply bruised heart hungered and panted after the Lord, and her first waking thought was a longing for His fellowship and presence. She kindled the same hunger in me. Remember, I had a bruised heart, too.

She read Philippians with me. And Ellis's marginal notes.

"This one thing I do" — how it smote home because this precept was lived out before my eyes. I marked it in my Bible, too.

"Rejoice always" — Edna had attained to that. How could I ever learn the secret? I marked the verse, but decided to try for Philippians 4:11 as more within the possibility of attainment: "For I have learned, in whatsoever state I am, therewith to be content." This became my life verse for the next ten years or so.

"That I may know him, and the power of his resurrection, and the fellowship of his sufferings, being made conformable unto his death" (Phil. 3:10). Great words that moved me to the depths of my being — I was on that quest. Little did I know, beyond that mere fact, that my feet were on the High Way. I was searching for Him.

CHAPTER SIX

EXTINGUISHED TAPERS

Who extinguishes their taper
Till they hail the rising sun?
Who discards the garb of winter
Till the summer has begun?
ANONYMOUS

It will doubtless astonish some adult readers, and perhaps make them shake their heads dubiously, to reveal that all this time I was still indulging in theaters, dances, and other worldly things. My father had long years before urged me to separate myself from these amusements, but my mother felt he was narrow in his views on such matters, and that they did no harm if indulged with discrimination. So I had gone along with her viewpoint as the easier and more pleasant.

Occasionally I wondered about it, but I was always sharply conscious of that old taunt, "You do this, or believe this, because your papa told you so." I was not going to give up any habit just because some human being told me to! If God told me to stop them I would obey. Otherwise I would continue as I had been.

These amusements were like the "taper" of our verse. They formed the light moments of my life, and I wasn't going to give up any fun just because some old religious fogey was prejudiced against it!

The first taper that I extinguished was card playing. In McMillan's boardinghouse the young folk often played until past midnight. If they had the ability, they put up some small stakes. I suppose the sailors thought a game inane if it did not have the element of gain or loss to stimulate them. I hesitated, more from reluctance to waste time and my precious pennies than for any other reason.

"Maybe Isobel doesn't think she should play cards, because she is religious," offered Jack gravely. Jack was one of the sailors, but very open to counsel. He even asked me to teach him the Bible at one time, and I believe he would have accepted the Lord if his wife and the others had not pulled him away.

I grabbed at this offer of a legitimate excuse in order to get out of such invitations easily. "Well, to tell the truth, Jack, I would prefer not to," I answered.

"Then we're not going to tease her into it," Jack informed everybody. "You play the piano for us, Isobel! We'd like some music while we play cards."

I loved to play the piano and preferred hymns above everything else. Those young people did not object to my religious selections, so the strange anomaly took place night after night. They played cards and gambled while I played from my hymn book. This left me free to go to bed as early as I liked.

This arrangement pleased me well. But having given up card playing, supposedly for religious reasons, I must in consistency hold to it on other occasions. So I did just that. It cost me nothing. I always thought cards were a tiresome waste of good mental energy. They achieved nothing but amusement, and I did not find them very amusing. So out went the taper of card playing.

It was during the summer of 1923, perhaps before I

went to The Firs, that I had to extinguish a second taper. This was quite a different affair and one about which no human being had ever spoken to me.

I was a voracious reader of romantic fiction. Novels gripped me and were my favorite mental escape from trials and difficulties, or from an evening which had to be spent alone. With a good love story I was immediately transported into another world. If the plot was exciting I could not put the book down until I finished it.

We were living with my brother on his ranch for the summer. As there were no other young people around, I had to occupy many evenings. I found a good novel was my first resort. This particular time, it was an exciting story that I could not lay down. I never did read the modern sexy novels, but chose clean, exciting love stories. Very often these were not really true to life. Life does contain moments of adventure, but these times are interspersed with long periods of plain, unvarnished hard work. The real things of life are attained at these monotonous level periods, so to speak, more than they are at the high peaks of excitement. People who feed on the lurid and melodramatic in their reading are not prepared for the long stretches of routine work which fill every life.

I believe this is partly responsible for many broken marriages today. Young people think married life should be all moonlight and thrills, and they balk when they find themselves on the level stretches of plain, ordinary working together, which actually are the real life and backbone of a home.

Anyway, I was deep in the excitement of the book. Midnight came and I was so near the end that I could not stop. In fact, it was one o'clock in the morning before I finished the book and took up my Bible for evening devotions. But I got no blessing from it. Never had the Bible seemed so drab and dull. When I tried to pray, the Lord seemed far away. It's just sleepiness, I told myself, and curled up for slumber.

But the next morning things were little better. God still seemed far away and the Bible stuffy and uninteresting. Before the Teachers' Summer Institute opened I was clerking in a Bible Depot which belonged to my father. He had felt that Victoria lacked a Christian bookstore. So, supported by Christian friends, he had opened this Bible Depot as a sideline. I substituted for the clerk while she was on summer vacation.

Traveling into town by bus gave me time to think. What had happened to me, that the Lord seemed no longer real? And why had the Bible, which I had begun to read through from Genesis to Revelation for the first time in my life — why had the Bible become insipid? I was alarmed. Sitting in the bus, I talked to the Lord about it in my heart.

"Oh Lord, what is wrong with me?" I prayed. "Why can't I sense Your presence now as I have lately? Why has the Bible become dry?"

"When a child fills her stomach with ice cream and soda pop," the Lord seemed to answer, "why does she lose her appetite for meat and potatoes?"

"Lord, do You mean the novel did that to me?"

"It excited all the fleshly part of your nature, didn't it? Did it do anything to help you spiritually?"

"Nothing, Lord. It kept me up so late. I'm tired this morning. Lord, if I promise to give up novel reading, will You come back to me? Will the Bible come alive to me again?"

"Try it and see."

From that moment, the Lord was real and present once more, and the Word took on new meaning. My spiritual growth could have been traced by the markings in that Bible as I read it from cover to cover. I discovered verses that seemed to spring out of the page as

His voice to meet my need at the moment. One verse I remember particularly. "For the mountains shall depart and the hills be removed, but my kindness shall not depart from thee, neither shall the covenant of my peace be removed, saith the Lord that hath mercy on thee" (Isa. 54:10). I have claimed this verse through the years, and it has been fulfilled to me.

I hardly need say that the taper of novel reading, which included magazine stories, was extinguished from that day on. For about fifteen years I never permitted myself to read a love story. After that, when I had to be alone in Lisuland so often, with problems pressing upon me, I used to read a bit at mealtimes, usually the old classics of Dickens, Thackeray, Brontë, and Barrie. These I had read before so they had no hold on me to continue reading past mealtime. And they did give me a wholesome mental holiday for an hour, lifting me out of the canyon world back into life among my own race.

Did I find it hard to make this self-denial? Does one miss candlelight when morning sunshine is pouring in the window? No, I was richly repaid for this self-discipline.

The next taper that the Lord touched was my dancing. Mac continued to invite me to the big university dances and to some of the smaller ones occasionally. It was at one of the latter — probably a fraternity dance — that I ran into Marion in the dressing room. Marion was a Christian girl in our year who had abstained all through her course from worldly amusements. We had both graduated now, and here we met at a dance!

"Why, Marion!" I exclaimed in surprise.

"Well, you are to blame, Isobel Miller," she said with her merry frankness. "You are the reason I am here tonight. You are a Christian, too, aren't you? And all through our four years you danced and had a good time while I got left out of everything. People say you are a good Christian, but you dance, so I decided to dance, too. This is my first dance."

I did not know it at the moment, but this was my last dance. I do not know how Marion ended up, but I fear she drifted from the Lord.

For one memorable dance I had as partner a science major named Keith. I had known him since high school days. As we were waltzing around he made some contemptuous remark about "old-fashioned fogies who believe in God."

Ah, I said to myself, here is my chance to witness. I always felt that if I kept in touch with the dancing crowd, it would afford me contacts for Christ with people who would not be contacted otherwise. So I started in eagerly, "Keith, why do you say that? I believe in God, and you used to."

"Oh, that was before I met Dr. Sedgewick or studied science," he replied impatiently. "No one with a scientific approach to life believes that old stuff any more."

"Oh, but they do!" I cried eagerly. "I have been investigating God and have indubitable proof that He exists!"

"What proof?" he scoffed.

I tried to tell him, but he refused to believe. He got angry, and we were arguing together hotly when a ripple of laughter brought us to ourselves. The orchestra had stopped playing, the dancers had taken their seats. Only Keith and I were left on the floor. Unconscious that the number had ended, we were waltzing round and round in the center of the room obviously fighting over something.

"Better give up, Keith!" called out a pal from the sidelines. "A woman convinced against her will is of the same opinion still. They never give in, and they don't know how to reason!"

When Keith saw what a laughingstock we had made of ourselves he swore angrily, marched me to a seat and stalked off in high dudgeon. If there is one thing a man can't forgive, it is a wound to his pride. I had caused Keith a public humiliation, and he cut me dead from that hour. My testimony to him had not only been a failure, it had left him more antagonistic than ever.

It was a very subdued and thoughtful Isobel whom Mac saw home that night. Was this the Lord speaking to me? I had led Marion astray. I had further antagonized Keith. Was dancing worth this?

A few nights later Mac telephoned me and asked me to the Agricultural Ball — in April, I think it was to be.

"Mac, I'm not sure," I parried. "That is so far ahead. Call me a little later, will you?" I would need to pray about it before going to another dance. Was this only an accident, or was the Lord speaking to me about giving up this amusement?

I was in the throes of indecision when the telephone rang again. A cheery voice with a rippling laugh called me from the other end. "Guess who is speaking, Isobel?" Only one person had such a contagious, delightful approach.

"Mrs. Whipple!" I cried in joy, almost trying to jump into the receiver. "Are you in town? Can I get to see you?"

"That you may," was the answer. "We are here on some business for a day or two and staying with Mrs. Ernest Walsh. Can you come out, or shall we come to you?"

McMillan's boardinghouse was no place for a quiet discussion. "Oh, I'll come to you," I replied. "Tell me how to get there."

Inside of an hour I was in the parlor of Mrs. Walsh's home, seated on a stool at Mrs. Whipple's feet. It was the most wonderful feeling just to be near her again!

Mr. Whipple was one with her, but had a shy silent disposition which took time and experience to appreciate. She often appealed to him for his opinion, however, and it was always worth waiting for.

"Well, tell me what you have been doing since the conference," she said gaily.

"That is just what I want to do," I answered, "for I have a pressing problem. Just before you called, a boyfriend phoned to ask me to the Aggie dance, and I put him off but told him I'd tell him definitely a little later. I'm all in a stew about it." Then I told her of my adventure with Keith.

Mrs. Whipple was probably scandalized to see that the girl she thought had been led into full consecration was still deep in worldly amusements, but she didn't show it. To have looked shocked at my doings would have made me resentful. Wasn't I honestly seeking the Lord and His will? I was merely refusing to act on *Your papa and your mama told you so.*

Mrs. Whipple gave a significant glance at her husband, then answered me sweetly. "I can quite see that you are in a mess, Isobel. You are trying to serve two masters at one time, and it always has painful results. Let's see what the Word of God says." She opened her Bible to I Corinthians 6:12 and read: "'All things are lawful unto me, but all things are not expedient.' You are compromising, Isobel, and that is fatal whatever realm it occurs in. Have you ever told Mac that you have become a Christian?"

"Oh, no," answered this product of the twentieth century. "Our set doesn't do that. It is a point of honor among us not to thrust our religious opinions upon the other fellow. I've never told anyone! It is my private life with God."

Poor Mrs. Whipple! What a warped little human being she had to deal with! But she was full of faith and of the Holy Ghost.

"Those are standards of your old life, Isobel," she said gently. "II Corinthians 5:17 says that 'if any man be in Christ, he is a new creature: old things are passed away behold all things are become new.'"

What a lovely verse! It sounded as if it had been written just for me. Then and there I marked it in my Bible.

"But look at II Corinthians 6:14-17, Isobel," went on my dear spiritual mother. "'Be ye not unequally yoked together with unbelievers . . . What communion hath light with darkness? . . . Wherefore come out from among them and be ye separate, saith the Lord.' That is the basis of our separation from things of the world and standards of the world. I Peter 3:15 says that we should be ready always to give a reason of the hope that is in us. I think it is your duty, under the standards of your new life with God, to tell your friends about Christ and what He has done for you. You will be surprised at the spiritual blessing it will bring."

"But I did try to tell Keith," I wailed, simply terrified at this idea of witnessing.

"But look at the place you were in when you told him," went on Mrs. Whipple. "You stood in the place of compromise and worldliness and then expected him to respect your testimony. No wonder he despised it. But now if you take your stand against dancing as belonging to your old life and unsuitable to the new, I believe you will find Mac showing a different reaction."

"Well, I'll try," I said dully. Young people always think that the older folk don't understand their generation. Inwardly I felt this way at the moment and dreaded speaking plainly to Mac. He had been so kind to me. I shrank from offending him or rendering myself odious in his eyes as I had done to Keith.

All the next day I dreaded that evening phone call,

and when the moment came I went cold all over and was nearly paralyzed with fright. But I gritted my teeth and took up the receiver. It was Mac, all right.

"Well, Isobel," he said. "What is the decision about the Aggie ball?"

My throat was so dry I could hardly get the words out. "Mac," I answered, "I hope you will forgive me, but I have become a Christian lately and have decided to give up dancing altogether. I do not criticize the gang in this matter, but I have had some experiences which make me feel that God would not have me continue to dance. I'm sorry not to have told you before — I was just undecided."

There was a long silence at the other end, during which my heart beat so violently I was afraid he could hear it. I was trembling from head to foot.

At length Mac's voice came over the wire. "Thank you, Isobel, for being so straightforward with me. I honor you for not playing with me about this. May I have the pleasure of your company to the baccalaureate service on Sunday instead?"

"Oh, thank you, Mac!" I said. "Yes, indeed. I would be delighted to go with you."

"It's a date, then. I'll call for you at nine-thirty. Good-bye."

I staggered to my room and fell across my bed in the weakness of relief. Mrs. Whipple had been right after all. Mac had said he honored me for being straightforward! And to prove it he had asked for another date immediately! Oh, how good of the Lord to let it happen that way. How did Mrs. Whipple know?

She knew the general principles of life, that compromise wins respect from no one, but a straightforward testimony does. Clean-cut action does, too. The older generation may not understand all the new scientific terms of the young generation, but they know the principles of life which never change. It is a wise young person who will not discard the inheritance of wisdom and experience from those who have gone before.

So the taper of dancing was extinguished and forgotten very quickly as the Rising Sun flooded my life with new and fascinating interests.

There remained just one taper now, the theater. I had gone only to good movies, an occasional classic opera, or wholesome family theater acts. There could be no harm in such, I thought, and they taught one much of human nature.

The last one I went to was a sweet, harmless story. I think it was Smilin' Thro'. I enjoyed it very much, but as I went home, once more all the old longings for romance and storybook experiences flooded me. The music, too, had stirred up the emotional side of me and once more prayer was a blank and the Bible had lost its savor. In vain I tried to push through to the Lord's presence. "My Beloved had withdrawn Himself and was gone" was as true of me as of the little bride in the Song of Solomon. "I sought Him, but I could not find Him; I called Him, but He gave me no answer." Later, when I read the Song of Solomon and came to this incident, I knew what it meant, perfectly. I had been there myself, for the second time.

"Oh, Lord," I prayed. "If You will but return to me I will never go to the theater again. You may have that also."

"It was but a little that . . . I found him whom my soul loveth: I held him and would not let him go" (Song of Solomon 3:4).

Nothing was worth the loss of fellowship with Him. Then did the Sun of Righteousness arise in my heart with healing in His wings.

I remember only once being tempted to relight this last taper. Remember how alone I was, how young, how accustomed to having many friends of my own age. It was an evening, perhaps in May, when everything in youth was calling for companionship and fun. The McMillan young folk were all going out together to see a movie and I would be left alone in the house.

"Oh, come on, Isobel," they teased, catching me by the hand. "It's a good clean movie tonight — can't possibly do you any harm. What does a young girl like you want to mope in the house for on such a lovely evening? Be companionable — come on with us!" They were a kindhearted group, and I was sorely tempted to go. The perfumed May air called to me from the open doorway. I was about to yield when I saw a doubtful look in Jack's eyes.

"Don't press her to do what she doesn't feel is right," he said quietly. That settled it.

"No, thank you," I returned. "Have a good time!" and waved them gaily off, then turned to go upstairs with a heavy heart. I entered my room, drab, rather dark, with its cheap furniture, and cried into the silence of the empty house, "Oh, Lord, is it to be so dull always? And I'm still young! A girl looks her nicest at twenty-one or two. Nobody to go with! Nothing to do but Bible study! Oh Lord, speak to me!" And I pulled over my Bible and opened it at random.

The words on the page sprang up before me. "Then said Jesus unto the twelve, Will ye also go away? Then Simon Peter answered him, Lord to whom shall we go? thou hast the words of eternal life" (John 6:67-68).

I sat there reading and re-reading that quiet, potent question. God did not refuse to let me go back to my earthly tapers. He just wanted me to think well before I did. Did I really prefer them? Would I change places with any one of the three girls who had just left the house? God forbid! I shrank from such a thought. Did I want to go back to Ben's world of loose loyalties? Again

I shuddered. Lord, to whom shall we go? There was no other road. The low road? Not for a moment. The Misty Flats? God deliver me from ever again drifting around there! Then there remained only The High Way.

"Forgive me, Lord." I bowed my head in contrition. "There is no one I want but Thee. Please comfort me." Then the sense of His Presence so filled the room that it is too sacred to talk about it. Suffice it to say that I never again looked back, but more and more learned the value of communion alone with Him.

Dr. Tozer has pointed out how our generation is in danger of missing this sacred joy. He says, "We have been trying to apply machine-age methods to our relations with God . . . our thought habits are those of the scientist, not those of the worshiper. We are more likely to explain than to adore." Searching is a scientific procedure, but we want to beware that it does not get into mechanical ruts. "We read our chapter, have our short devotions, and rush away, hoping to make up for our deep inward bankruptcy by attending another gospel meeting, or listening to another thrilling story told by a religious adventurer lately returned from afar."

We need to worship and to adore as well as to analyze and explain. Mary of Bethany learned much by just sitting at Jesus' feet, listening to Him and loving Him. Our generation's greatest lack is just here.

By the summer of 1924, unknown to me, my year in Arabia was over. Mac had gone out of the city on a summer job. When he returned I was in Chicago at Moody Bible Institute. We have never seen one another since. My Rising Sun had planned many things to fill the place of my extinguished tapers, but each was to be a separate and delightful discovery. Next on God's program for me was a contact which changed the whole course of my life.

CHAPTER SEVEN

J. O. FRASER OF LISULAND

When at the close of The Firs Conference in 1923, Mrs. Whipple lent me a book called *The Growth of a Soul*, she had no idea that for many years Dr. and Mrs. Isaac Page had been secretly praying God would lay His hand on Isobel Miller for missionary service in China. She did know, however, that in the life story of Hudson Taylor, founder of the China Inland Mission, were experiences of searching for God and proving Him which were parallel to some through which I was now passing.

Anyone who knows *The Growth of a Soul* will recognize the gold mine it was to me. Hudson Taylor went much deeper in his searchings, of course, and came out with definite maxims for life and conduct. "Learn to move man through God by prayer alone" was one of the many that I eagerly noted, and it has blessed me all my life.

By the time I had finished the book, one thing was clear to me: I wanted to belong to the mission that Hudson Taylor founded. I wanted to work with the group who had proved God in that quiet, unostentatious fashion.

Having finished *The Growth of a Soul*, I went on to read the second volume, *The Growth of a Work of God*, about the founding of the China Inland Mission. It was while reading this that I received a call to the field. Previously I had felt a call to the mission regardless of where it worked. But as I read of the sorrows and sufferings of Chinese women my heart was greatly stirred. I knew now what a heartache was. When I had been groping for a way out of spiritual darkness, my Bible was handy on my bookshelf. It was easy for me to find the way. But what about those who had never heard of Christ? No matter how willing they might be to follow Him fully, they must perish unless someone went and told them. If they only knew of Him and of His death for their salvation! How shall they believe in him of whom they have not heard? and how shall they hear without a preacher? (Rom. 10:14). I knew I must go and tell them. So when I arrived at The Firs in 1924, my decision to apply to the China Inland Mission had already been made.

No one needed to give up a pair of shoes to bring me to the conference for the second time. I had been saving money during the year and had also applied for the position of waitress to earn my board while there.

I was simply thrilled to be back at the beloved place. I ran, almost flew, from spot to spot of hallowed memory. The cabin which Edna Gish (now back in China) and I had shared, the spot in among the tall fir trees where I had often prayed alone, the open-air auditorium where our classes had met, the original Firs cabin with the big fireplace where we had held such blessed times of testimony — I wanted to see them all. Last in my inspection tour was this old cabin. I dashed in eagerly and was halfway to the center of the room before I could check my impulsive entrance. For it was not empty. One lone occupant, a middle-aged gentleman, was sitting there by himself. He smiled at my surprise, and I tried to apologize while backing out as speedily as I could.

Some old bachelor, I told myself, and flew off to look at the kitchen. How I sensed that he was unmarried, I do not know. Maybe it was a certain lonely, wistful look in his eyes. Anyway, I promptly forgot him in the joy of greeting other arrivals and getting into the swing of the waitress routine, which was new to me. Little did I dream that I had just met one who was to be a spiritual lodestar to me and to the dear husband God was planning to give me but of whose existence I, as yet, knew nothing.

It was not until the evening meeting that, to my intense surprise, I found that the "old bachelor" of the sitting-room loneliness was seated on the platform and being introduced as our principal speaker for the conference — Mr. J. O. Fraser of the China Inland Mission. I had never heard of him before, and apparently neither had anyone else. Even Mr. Whipple probably did not know at the time that this young Englishman was an honors graduate of London University in electrical engineering and a brilliant pianist. He appeared among us as a simple missionary and never by word or action gave any hint of his extraordinary gifts.

When he got up to speak, he told us simply how the CIM had sent him to one of the farthest corners of China, to the border of Burma and Yunnan Province. There he had worked among the Chinese for several years, but had frequently noticed a people coming into the market who were not Chinese at all. They did not speak Chinese among themselves, and they did not dress like the Chinese. They wore turbans, and their clothing, especially that of the women, was very colorful and trimmed with cowrie shells and silver bangles. They knew some trade-language Chinese, and through this he discovered that they were Lisu tribespeople who lived in the mountains of the Salween River canyon. They had never heard of the Lord Jesus Christ, and their language had never been reduced to writing. They were entirely illiterate. Moreover, they were not idol worshippers like the Chinese, but animists who worship demons. God called him to go to these people with the gospel.

Since he was scheduled to speak several evenings during the conference, Mr. Fraser told us of a different phase of work among the Lisu each night. For instance, one night he took us itinerating over those wonderful alpine mountains, climbing great heights to where small villages perched — precariously, it often seemed — on the edge of abysmal ravines. He told of the language difficulties — how he learned it from living with the people in their smoky little shacks, how he reduced it to writing, and how with two colleagues he was led to form what is now called the Fraser Script.

Another evening he stressed the patience needed in teaching the older folk, illiterate from their youth. He was full of humor, and his descriptions of the old ladies who declared they had no power of memory and then were tricked by him into relating with detail what had happened to their children fifteen years ago, were simply hilarious — and touching. We learned to love those old women.

One lecture was on the spiritual battle in the heavenlies — how he roughed it, and labored, and had given them a written language — and still there were so few converts. And those who did come were not stable. Then he wrote his mother in England to gather in the neighbors and pray. It was only after this prayer group began to function in earnest that "the break" came in the Lisu tribe. At that time he, on the field, had been led to resist in Christ's name the devil and his host who were holding this tribe enchained.

As I sat listening I saw plainly that it was true — the Lisu church had been born in prayer travail. I decided that I must also employ this weapon of "all-prayer." It is so obviously effective and is attainable to any of us. I received a life pattern at that moment for which I have ever been grateful.

Another evening was given over to the joys of harvest. He took us on a trip with him, and his descriptions were so vivid that we were simply transported out of America to the mountainous banks of the Salween canyon. We saw him dressed in the costume of a Chinese coolie, lest better clothes detract from his message. With a Lisu carrier or guide, he climbed the steep approach to one of these high villages. He cupped his hands to his mouth and gave the Lisu call: "Ma-pa chi la-o!" (The male teacher is arriving!) At this all the dogs of the village rushed out and down the path at them. Then followed the banging of doors and merry shouts as the brightly colored costumes of the women flashed back and forth, and the menfolk darted forward to drive off the dogs. The Christians lined up to shake hands, and as the tall missionary went down the line, each woman managed to stick an egg into his hand as she gave the handshake of welcome! They had learned that he liked eggs, so he always had to carry a bag over his shoulder to hold the eggs, fresh and ancient, which such a visit collected!

He told of the Prophet's Chamber behind the chapel. The Christian villagers had built it for him on learning that queerest trait of the white man, that he liked privacy sometimes! Imagine wanting to be alone! Eh, eh, how queer! Perhaps it came from the color of his skin. But if he wanted privacy he should have it. So he had a little "prophet's chamber" of his own in each village.

Then would start the catechizing for baptism. He told of going to call the next candidate and finding the man on his face, prostrate in prayer, asking his new-found Savior to help him answer correctly, so that he might be adjudged ready for this solemn step.

And so on.

The last night Mr. Fraser said he needed more missionaries — young men of consecration, willing for the privations and loneliness such a life entailed.

Down in my seat in the side aisle my heart thrilled with love for the Lisu people. Inwardly I prayed, "Lord, I'd be willing to go. Only I'm not a man."Never did the vision of the Lisu tribe leave me. I dared not name it a call, but I believe that time has proved it was.

My father was with me at The Firs that summer. As it happened, he was Mr. Fraser's cabin mate. To my surprise, I found out that Father had invited Mr. Fraser to come and stay with us in Victoria for a week before he sailed for China in August. That summer we had rented a house at Oak Bay near the beach and had a room for a visitor.

I was amazed at Father's temerity in inviting Mr. Fraser without consulting Mother. At that time, she and my brother were both opposed to my going as a missionary to China. Mother was not likely to be pleased at bringing a CIM missionary into her home when she was trying to influence me to be content with Christian work in America!

But I was thrilled at the possibility of having a private talk with Mr. Fraser about missionary service. I was hoping to go to Moody Bible Institute that autumn, but the obstacles in my way were so many that I sometimes wondered if they could be from the Lord. I was Mother's only daughter. How important was that?

I had made up my mind during those evening talks on Lisuland that this unknown missionary was a great man of God. His gifts, apart from his platform ability, were still hidden and unknown to me, but the man himself was obviously walking closely with the Lord. It was one of the thrills of my life in later years to discover that many others, far more capable of judging such matters than I, also acclaimed him as one of the great spiritual men of his generation. He is, of course, the hero of the book, *Behind the Ranges*, written by Mrs. Howard Taylor many years after his death.

Come he did, and by his simple sincerity and kindly interest won the admiration of both my mother and brother. My mother had been a musician before her marriage. She composed music and often wrote the lyrics too. None of her pieces had ever been refused by any publisher to whom she offered them. She did not go on with this after marriage, that was all. It was in seeking for a contact with Mother that Mr. Fraser suddenly revealed his brilliance at the piano. Mother was enthralled. They "talked music." Mother knew the names of his teachers and said he had been taught by some of the best masters in London.

I was watching for a chance to present my own problems. It came later in the week. Mr. Fraser wanted to see the beach and I was appointed to take him down one afternoon. We were no sooner alone than I told him I had wanted to speak with him about my missionary call. We sat down on the sands by a rocky bit of shore, and I told him. I have never forgotten that session.

"Missionary life can be very lonely," he said quietly. He proceeded to unfold some of his own early sufferings. I believe now that he did it deliberately to sift me. f I were truly called of God, I would not be discouraged by plain talk about the cost. If I were not called by God, but just had romantic notions of a foreign land, the sooner my gossamer dream wafted away the better.

He little knew the unveiling of his own life that he was giving unconsciously. In fact, as he reminisced he seemed to forget for a while that I was present. His blue-gray eyes brooding out over the sunny, sparkling ocean, he seemed almost to be talking to himself. In the quiet of contemplation, as now, his eyes seemed to reveal an understanding of all the sorrows and loneliness that a human heart can know. Acquainted with grief, they were sad eyes. Knowing the victory possible, they were steadfast and patient.

I told him of Mother's viewpoint and her opposition to my call. He answered with the slow drawl which was his when thinking out a question — none could talk faster than he on occasion. "I have sensed that Satan is opposing you and working through your mother and your brother. We are taught 'whom resist' when it come to obstacles produced by the devil. I think that should be your stand. In prayer resist the devil, always remembering to be kind to those who are unconsciously his tools at the moment (2 Timothy 2:24). I have a prayer formula which I use on such occasions. It is this: If this obstacle be from Thee, Lord, I accept it. But if it be from Satan, I refuse him and all his works in the name of Calvary. I have found that this formula works." I was to use it throughout my life and never found it to fail when prayed with the honest intention of obeying all that it implied.

Again Mr. Fraser brooded out over the ocean thoughtfully, then added, "I wonder if you will ever get to China. You are very young, and you have great obstacles to face." He lapsed into a reverie for a few moments, then began to talk as if he knew what to say. "It is even conceivable that after you get to Bible school, Satan will attempt to get you away. For instance, a telegram might come saying that your mother was very sick and urging you to return home immediately. Now, if that should happen, you cannot leave the moment you get the telegram. You would have to pack your trunk and buy a ticket, and these things take time. Is there any Christian in Vancouver or here whom you can trust to be unprejudiced and yet godly enough to discern such a matter and be able to advise you?"

"There is Mr. Charles Thomson, district secretary of the CIM," I answered.

"The very man!" he replied quickly. "If you get such a telegram, wire immediately to Mr. Thomson, asking him to check just how ill your mother is. By the time your trunk is packed you should have his reply, and can then see more clearly the path the Lord would have you take."

I listened in awe, but would have been still more amazed if I had known how exactly that prophecy was to be fulfilled.

He that is spiritual judgeth all things (I Cor. 2:15).

It was an afternoon well spent. Upon the plastic material of a young life had been imprinted standards and ideals which were to last forever. And a deep glimpse had been afforded me into the life that is hidden in God — the cost of it, the fragrance of it, and the power of it.

CHAPTER EIGHT

THE MOODY BIBLE INSTITUTE

September 3, 1924, found me in Chicago, enrolling as a student of the Bible missionary course at Moody Bible Institute. This was a most unexpected turn of affairs and not the product of my own planning. I was so very Canadian in loyalty that I would never have chosen to come to the United States for my training. And I admired Professor Ellis so much that I would not have thought of looking beyond the Vancouver Bible School for my missionary preparation. But the Lord took the matter out of my hands.

At the end of the school year 1923-4 I still lacked funds to put me through any Bible school. Outside of my parents and one other person I told no one. God in His wondrous workings brought that one other person into contact with Miss Marjorie Harrison, whom I had met at The Firs. At that precise moment she was asking Him how to use some money she had saved, and inadvertently learned that I needed funds to train for China. It was Marjorie who chose Moody for me, directed by the Lord, I am sure.

Herself a graduate of the Bible Institute of Los Angeles and knowing of this small Bible school right in the city where I was living, she still chose to send me halfway across the continent to Chicago. The largest school of its kind in the country, Moody Bible Institute offered rich opportunity for many kinds of Christian work. This was what I needed more than I knew.

Marjorie explained that her money was limited to that little savings account. She would buy my ticket to Chicago, but could not help me with the return fare. She would pay my board and room for one year, but had no money for my incidental expenses. And she could not help me after that first year. The institute had an employment bureau to help students find jobs for odd hours in safe places. For the rest, I must trust the Lord. Was I willing?

Fresh from reading Hudson Taylor's experience in proving God able to supply his need through prayer only, I was thrilled with the opportunity to go on searching.

My brother had to make a business trip to Chicago at that time, so I had company across the continent. Dr. Isaac Page met us at the station and took me to the school. Otherwise, I knew no one in that big, whirling metropolis. The Pages had just recently moved to Chicago themselves as deputation workers for the China Inland Mission in the Midwest.

That first day of enrollment, with its trips to this office and that for registration, was bewildering. At the end of the day I was truly weary. I was put into a double room — cheaper than a single room — with a strange girl who was European and spoke with a strong accent. The furnishings were very simple, and the house opened right on the street. Being on the first floor front, we saw that people walking along the street passed right under our window. I had never lived in a house which did not have a front enclosure, and it gave me an exposed feeling to be so near a public street. This, added to the weariness and loneliness, made me homesick. Can I stand this for two years? I was asking myself, when a bus rumbled up to a stop at our corner.

To sleep with my head just the other side of a wall from such public things seemed almost scandalous. But in another moment I was swung into the heavenlies. The bus was the MBI street-meeting group, returning from their first evening's witness, and they had begun to sing.

He makes the path grow brighter
All along the way:
He makes the journey lighter
Every passing day.

Beautiful young voices in four-part harmony sung with a fervent faith in words that came right from their hearts; the singing thrilled me through and through. Something in the traffic held them there while they sang the hymn to a finish.

"Oh, Lord," I prayed in ecstasy, "thank You! Thank You! This is the other side of this 'exposed' existence comradeship in the things of Christ and in the cause of soul winning. And Christian friends who are my own age and can sing like that? Oh, thank You, Lord!" Truly transported into His presence, I nestled down in deep content and fell asleep.

More good things awaited me.

The next day I was called to the telephone. It was the Dean's office. "Miss Miller, there is a girl named Lillian Billington just arrived from Bellingham who would like to room with you. What is your pleasure in the matter?"

"Oh," I cried, "has she really come? Yes, please. I would like so much to be her roommate. I met her at The Firs. She is a young schoolteacher."

"Yes, that is right," answered the office voice, "but you will have to change your dormitory. We have Miss Billington down for the third floor, Ransom Hall

Building, Room 303. Will you kindly proceed to move there as soon as possible, and leave your present room in a proper state for a new occupant? Thank you. Report to us when the move is completed."

Room 303 Ransom Hall was much larger, higher above the street, much more private, and in every way a happier arrangement to my taste. Best of all, I was to share it with a girl from The Firs. We had just met the summer before, but I liked her sweet face. "Billie" and I were happy roommates for two years. Next door at 304 was a Scottish girl, Anne Barr — who years later was to be namesake to my daughter — and a very unselfish American girl, Ella Dieken, who was later to play a part in my life that the wildest dreams could never have conjured up.

What a meeting Billie and I had! And what fun to help her unpack and find that she had things I didn't — pretty curtains for our windows, cretonne drapes for our trunks, lacy dresser scarfs, and so on. Soon our room was transformed into a real girls' bower, and my beauty-loving soul was deeply grateful.

Mealtime was an adventure, with hundreds of students all eating at once. Oh the noise of the talk, the clatter of the cutlery and dishes! The men sat on one side of the dining room and the women on the other, twelve to a table. A senior and a junior student were assigned to the end seats, but the rest of us changed places each day. Two students at each table were appointed daily to bring in the food and carry the dishes out.

I was waiting in line one day for the hot vegetables. As soon as the bell rang, the food would be dished out to us, but there was still a moment before the hour struck. I was dreaming of Lisuland when, turning around suddenly, I encountered the eyes of another dreamer — the young man who ran the dishwashing machine. It was one of those shock encounters when you find yourself already over the threshold and into the other fellow's soul before there is time to knock for admission. Very embarrassing. Each of us looked away quickly and pretended not to notice, but it had happened. From then on I was conscious of that dishwasher! Whether he was a full-time kitchen employee or student help I did not know. The annoying thing was that I had become conscious of him.

I had made up my mind that I was not going to have any boyfriends at Moody. I had proved that they were distracting, and I wanted these two years to be given to unhindered preparation for my life work in China. So I was extremely cross with myself to find out that as soon as I entered the kitchen I looked every time to see if he was there or not. To discipline myself, I did not inquire his name or his status, but frequently I had to carry dishes past him, and I felt sure he knew my name and all about me.

I was correct: he did. But he never tried to speak. I did appreciate that. I did not know that he had come to the Bible Institute vowing to have nothing to do with girls, lest they distract him from his studies! But he had made inquiries as to who the girl was who wore the green blouse trimmed with brown swan's down.

Shortly after my arrival, Dr. and Mrs. Page invited me to supper in their apartment. He had long been my father's close friend, and I had called him Daddy Page for years. After I had taken off my wraps, he thrust a bundle of photographs of the institute and Moody students into my hands, excusing himself while he went to help his wife in the kitchen. As I looked over the pictures I came across one which greatly attracted me, the portrait of a girl who showed character as well as beauty.

"Oh, Daddy Page," I cried, "who is this? What a lovely face! Is she here at the institute?"

He came in and looked over my shoulder. "Oh that," he said. "Yes, Isobel. She is a lovely girl. Her name is Kathryn Kuhn, but she has just graduated and gone on to Wheaton College. I wish you could meet her. She has a brother here at the institute."

"Oh, yes?" I said politely, and quickly changed the conversation. Inwardly, I said, Well, if her brother looks like she does, I'll stay away from him. Here's where you don't go to any mixed parties, Isobel Miller!

Apart from the freshman reception, I quietly refused invitations to any party or picnic where young men would be present — that is, during my first term. It was my second term before I found out all this reserve had been in vain, for I learned that the dishwasher in the kitchen was the brother of Kathryn Kuhn!

Of my studies during those two years and four months (I was ill and lost a term) I can only glance at the blessing they brought me. Dr. James Gray was President then, and I was privileged to have a class under him. Bible Analysis under Dr. Robert Jaderquist was an outstanding joy, and I later passed it on to the Lisu church, analyzing First and Second Peter with our Bible school students. Those notes are still being used.

Dr. Elbert McCreery taught Comparative Religions and was one of my favorite teachers. He was himself the blessing, with his gentle, Christ-like life.

Dr. Robert Hall Glover made me sit on the edge of my seat in eagerness, week after week, as he presented the challenge of missions, and in another class taught the History of Missions. His fire continually kindled my own.

Talmage J. Bittikofer taught us part singing and conducting, which I was to use constantly with the Lisu church. We all loved "Bitti," and his solos stirred me to the depths.

I could go on, but I think the greatest help at Moody

came to me in the practical work assignments under the direction of Mrs. Frances C. Allison. Every student had to take one or more assignments each week. These assignments were changed each term, giving every student a great variety of experience.

Open-air meetings among the Jews would likely mean rotten eggs and tomatoes pelted at you, so you wore your oldest clothes. I was knocked off the sidewalk into the street once when my turn came for Jewish work. Sunday school classes and hospital or jail visitation were considered the easiest assignments, and my Lord started me off gently with these. A slip of paper from the Practical Work Department told me I was assigned to teach a Sunday school class and do visitation during the week in the Italian slums. I would work under senior student Miss Ethel Thompson, Room X, 830 Building, and would I please report to her immediately for instructions.

So behold a young Moody freshman climbing the stairs of the 830 Building and standing before a closed bedroom door, about to knock. What would Miss Thompson be like? How could I ever do slum visitation? How my heart beat as I firmly knocked at that door! Once it opened, I was in for it--that is, I must plunge into soul winning, from which my shyness had always shrunk.

The door was opened by a short, slim young woman, perhaps in her early thirties. When she heard my name, she welcomed me quickly with a soft, southern drawl. After asking me to sit down, she began. "I suppose I had better tell you about our assignment. We are working under a community house or church in the Italian quarter. The minister in charge is a modernist and conducts dances on Sunday evening, and so on. This is our big difficulty and the most discouraging feature. But we are in charge of the primary department on Sundays and have full liberty to preach the gospel there. They think we cannot 'hurt' the little ones!

"During the week we go into the homes — tenement houses — knock at doors, and present our message. The people are poor, of course, and many of them are Roman Catholics, but there have been a few decisions for Christ. Personally, I think the work needs prayer almost more than anything else."

"Tommy" (none of the students called her Ethel) eyed this new freshman questioningly, wondering what the Lord had sent her in me.

Remembering Mr. Fraser's lessons on the place of prayer in Christian service, I answered eagerly, "Oh, I believe in prayer too! I'd be happy to come over here to your room every day for a time of prayer together."

"Would you?" Tommy asked, her face lighting up with hope and joy. "All right. I'm working my way through school here, so I am busy, but half an hour before noon each day — how would that suit you?" It fit into my schedule and became an important part of my life.

That first Sunday, Tommy took me to the community center and introduced me as her new helper to the Rev. Mr. K–, the minister in charge. "Fine," he said. "How about having lunch with us today? I told the wife there would be a new worker and we ought to get acquainted, so she is prepared."

That meant our staying for the morning service. Mr. K– spoke about courage or high ideals or gave some such verbal essay, but there was nothing in it to bring new life to anyone.

After dinner in their apartment, he said to us rather patronizingly, "You know, girls, I used to believe like you do. In fact, you may be surprised to learn that I am a Bible school graduate myself. But after graduation I went into a seminary and there learned that no one nowadays believes in that old-fashioned stuff. I lost my 'faith,' as you call it, at seminary. But somehow our liberalism does not energize people like your teaching seems to, so when I found out how dead the work is here, I asked for a couple of Moody students to be sent us to stir up interest in the neighborhood. You bring them in, and we'll mold them into a good community!"

We stifled the comment that rose so quickly to our lips, and I said, "This is very strange, Mr. K–. You have departed from the old faith and I have just departed from liberalism to return to the faith! I lost my belief in God in college, but I have done some personal investigation in the matter, and I'm now convinced that He is, and the only way to Him is through faith in the atoning power of the blood of Christ to bring forgiveness of sins and eternal life. You and I are a contrasting pair. You have entered The Misty Flats while I have just found my way out of them back on to the High Way again."

Mr. K–'s eyes sparkled with interest, and he leaned forward, plying me with questions. He was sarcastic and argumentative, but evidently moved. Tommy sat quiet, praying. She had never heard my story, but recognized instantly the working of the Spirit of God.

When it came time to leave, Mr. K– was belligerent again. "You're too intelligent a girl to slip back into that old stuff," he challenged me. "We'll have to have some more talks about this! You girls must come to supper some night after your visitation work."

On the long car ride home Tommy said, "I believe God has already begun to answer our prayers. Just think of His sending a worker who had been through all this liberal stuff that is binding this man from any power really to help change lives! I watched his face while you talked, and many of your points went home, though he was too proud to acknowledge it. I have faith now to believe that God will bring Mr. K– back to the faith! Let us agree together on Matthew 18:19 and add this request to our daily prayers."

Tommy proved to be a most rare companion. She had a keen sense of humor, and droll wit simply poured from her. Visitation was in itself a grim experience for me. Those dark, dirty tenement houses, with broken stairs, bad plumbing which often made the place reek, and whole families cooped up in one small room sometimes, would have terrified me if I had been alone. But Tommy always had a merry retort or comment for a stubbed toe or an offended nose, a remark so pungent in its truth and applicability that I was shaken with laughter which often helped me overcome my distaste. She always took the brunt of the first attack, so to speak. She was an artist at tactful approach, and I sat at her feet and tried to learn.

More than thirty years have passed since those days, so I cannot remember details of her personal work conversations, or of her delightful wit. But I do remember one incident. In a long, dark hall of an old tenement house we were going from door to door, seeking entrance and opportunities for conversation. One door was opened by a big brute of a man who scowled at us and shouted, "What are you after? What ya doin' here?"

"Brother," Tommy smiled up at him with her soft, southern drawl, "we're a couple of friends who are interested in seeing that you get a better deal. Won't you let us come in and talk a moment?"

"Ah, come on," growled the man suspiciously." "Nobody's really interested in helping us. What's your life? Salesman? Politics? Whatever it is, we ain't interested," and he moved to the door as if to bang it in our faces.

"Now, brother," piped up Tommy plaintively, "a pair of poor tired girls can't hurt a big fellow like you.

Won't you even offer us a chair a moment? We've been on our feet for hours and we did hope —"

A woman's voice came from within, "They can sit down a moment, can't they, Bill? I know what it is to have tired feet."

Bill cursed bitterly, but left the door open. He turned and stalked to the far side of the dismal room. Tommy, with a droll remark about her feet, made the woman laugh, and a conversation was soon under way. The Lord's name was no sooner uttered, however, than Bill appeared in our midst again, eyes blazing with anger. "So it's religious sluts you are! That's the worst of all! I'm not going to have any blankety blank," he swore profusely, "whinings around here! I'm an atheist, I am" — and so on.

Tommy turned on her loving, merry humor. I do not know how she did it, except that the Spirit of God was working with her, but she had him quieted and listening before we left. If I remember rightly, his wife decided for Christ. Almost every visitation day, some soul made that decision for eternity. Dear Tommy. It was she who taught me that "loving folks" is the only way to approach them for the Lord Jesus Christ.

In the primary department of the church, also, God began to work. The children started to ask the Lord to come into their hearts. Mr. K– was interested and indifferent by turns. Sometimes he would ignore us for weeks, almost as if antagonistic. On other occasions he would come into our Sunday school and listen and watch and invite us around for a meal.

How we labored in prayer for this man! Tommy with her cute remarks in the dark hallways of tenement houses was one person. On her knees praying for the salvation of souls and the reclamation of Mr. K–, she was quite a different person. Yet the two sides of her character blended into one another. If you heard only her jokes, you would never have guessed at her tears and her passionate pleadings for sin-bound souls

In my second term I asked to be reappointed to the same assignment. Tommy and I both felt the Lord's work was not completed in that place. But that was the term I fell ill and lost six weeks of study. Of course I could not go with Tommy. At the end of that term she graduated and left for Mexico.

But there is one precious thing yet to record.

After I came out of the infirmary and just before Tommy left the institute, we were both called down to the reception room one day. To our surprise, it was Mr. K–. He was a changed man and his face wore a gentle, chastened look. There was a light there we had never seen before.

"I am calling on you girls to tell you that the Lord has answered your prayers for me," he said. "I have come back to Him. It has been a bitter fight, as you doubtless have watched and seen. Pride refused to be crucified for a long time. But week by week it became more evident to me that the Word you girls preached was the power of God unto salvation. Lives were changed through your ministry; my honesty had to admit it. Nobody was changed through mine.

"Maybe you don't know that I began to preach the Bible again when I saw how God used your Bible teaching. But nothing happened. Then I had to come to the place where I was willing to preach the cross of Christ as the only way, the blood of the Redeemer as the only atonement for our sins. The preaching of the cross worked — for me as well as for you. There has been an awful fuss. I made a confession in the pulpit and stopped the Sunday dances. Attendance picked up, the church was filled for services, but the committee got wind of what I had done and were very angry." Tears came into his eyes. "In short, they dismissed me. But I have a little country church appointment now and will be moving out there with my family. And I can preach the truth there. My wife is wholeheartedly with me, and we both feel we have to thank you two. God bless you. And God bless the school that D. L. Moody founded."

With tears in our eyes and awe in our hearts we said a hearty "amen."

We did not see Mr. K– again.

CHAPTER NINE
SPIRITUAL PREVISION

In December 1924 I received a letter from my mother saying that she was facing the possibility of undergoing a surgical operation. It was discovered that she had a tumor, and there was a choice before her: radiology treatments over quite a long period of time, or surgery. She was inclined toward surgery as being less drawn out, to get it over with instead of making the many long trips to town which the radiology would necessitate.

I had not heard definitely what her decision had been when a telegram arrived saying she was with the Lord. She had chosen surgery and had died in the hospital following the operation. Father wired me lovingly, but said the funeral would be over before I could reach home, so I should not try to come.

This was a shattering blow to me. My mother had opposed my going to the foreign field because of her clinging love for me, her only daughter. In the agony of her pleadings with me she had said some bitter things which at the time I had not taken to heart. I had recognized that they were the upflinging of violent emotion and not the result of considered thought. But one word had been: "You are praying to go to China, and God answers prayer, but you will go only over my dead body." That memory now came back to me and simply lacerated my heart.

I owe a great deal to my mother. With her deep affections she held high ideals and was very conscientious. She sacrificed her musical career and many opportunities for a musical evening with other young people in order to baby-sit with her two children at home. She married young and was still in her twenties when my brother and I were born. She had great ambitions for her children and carefully watched over us. We were never allowed to run the streets. She gave up her evenings to reading to us and planning to make home a pleasant place where our friends were welcome. She was a Christian, at one time a consecrated Christian, and always trained us to love the Lord and honor His Word. As we grew older she wanted us "to move in good society," and this was the temptation which had led her to compromise with worldly things. But at the root of it was her natural love for us.

I had taken my mother's love for granted, accepting the warmth of the daily sunshine in such careless security that I had not shown her the gratitude which was her due. All these things came back to me now that she was gone, but it was too late to express my thanks to her and my heart was sorely torn.

During that Christmas vacation I took employment as a waitress in a restaurant. School reopened in January.

One day in class a messenger went up to the platform and handed the teacher a note. He read it and said, "Will Miss Isobel Miller please go to the office of the Dean of Women? There is a telegram for you."

Astounded and wondering, I got up and sped toward the Women's Building. What could it be? I was trembling by the time I reached the office, and from the Dean's face I knew it was bad news of some kind. I could only look at her in agony and beg that she tell me quickly and not prolong suspense. She did so. "Sit down, dear," she said. "The telegram reads: FATHER CRITICALLY INJURED IN ELEVATOR ACCIDENT. COME HOME AT ONCE. MURRAY. Who is Murray?"

"My brother," I choked out. "Oh, but I can't stand it. Father too! Oh—!"

"Is there anyone we can call to help you, dear?" she asked tenderly.

Suddenly in imagination I was far away, sitting on a seaside beach beside a tall, strong man who was looking out over the breaking sea with brooding eyes. He was saying, "Satan may try to get you away from the institute. Is there anyone you know who can be depended on for godly, unprejudiced judgment?" In a flash I recognized that Mr. Fraser's foresight had been an exact premonition in all except one detail. He had thought it would be Mother, but it turned out to be my brother who summoned me home. The memory of Mr. Fraser's advice steadied and quieted me.

Sitting up straight, I said, "Yes, please, I would like Dr. Isaac Page to come and help me."

The dean was relieved to be able to do something, and in a moment she was talking to him on the telephone. I waited in the dean's office until he arrived — my father's intimate friend.

"Daddy Page," I said, "Mr. Fraser told me this might happen. He also told me what to do if it did happen. I will go and pack my trunk, but will you please do two things for me? Reserve a ticket for the train tonight, but don't buy it yet. Will you please wire immediately to Mr. Charles Thomson and ask if Dad is as bad as Murray said?"

"Excellent idea, Isobel," Dr. Page said. "First reports of these accidents are often excited and exaggerated. Mr. Thomson will know. I will go and do that immediately. There is no train going to Vancouver until this evening, anyway. And you? You will trust and not be afraid?"

"Yes," I said, much calmer now that a plan of activity was under way. "Thank you. Everyone here is so kind and loving to me. I will be all right."

"I'll come back just as soon as I have wired and made the train reservation," he said, and was gone.

Before supper that evening the answering telegram arrived. It read: FATHER IMPROVING SENDS LOVE AND SAYS STAY AT YOUR POST. WRITING. THOMPSON.

Oh, what a relief! The letter that followed told how the elevator girl had lost control and the cage had crashed four stories to the cement basement. Daddy was injured internally, and the jar began a trouble which did finally take his life, but he lived for nearly twenty happy years before that took place!

"He that is spiritual judgeth all things" (I Cor. 2:15).

How did Mr. Fraser know this might happen? When God's child is living close to Him and perfectly yielded to His will, it is possible to spread his mind out in the Lord's presence and catch the instruction of God. This is especially true if interceding for someone else. If there were no God this could not be. Satan can read man's thought and describe the past, he can use intelligence and guess at the future, but he cannot *know* the future.

This experience was followed closely by another special instance of the Spirit's operation.

The Otis Whipple family were no longer in Seattle, but in China. Mr. Whipple, a fine architect, had been called to build a missionary hospital in one of the big inland cities. He took his family with him, so it was some time before Mrs. Whipple heard of my sorrows.

One day I received a letter from her. It said something like this. "Isobel, I feel your mother was spiritually prepared to go home. It was very strange. I knew nothing of the possibility of her operation, let alone her danger, but on the day of her death I was so burdened for her that I spent a long time in prayer and had assurance that she was at last yielded to God's will in all things.

"But now as I write I have another burden that presses upon me. It is for you, and somehow connected with your father. I am in much prayer for you, dear, and for him. I do not know what is happening, but God has called me today to intercede for you both, and claim only His will to be done upon each of you."

I looked at the date of Mrs. Whipple's letter. It was the very day the telegram came telling of Father's accident. Mrs. Whipple was in inland China, halfway around the world, with no human knowledge whatever of what had taken place. She could not possibly have known, for I did not learn it myself for several months, that before she went to the hospital Mother admitted that I had chosen the better course in pursuing the will of God. What had been worldly ambition in her life she confessed to Him and before she died she came back to her earlier consecration of all to the Lord. Who knows how much Mrs. Whipple's intercession helped to win that battle?

I was deeply impressed, wistfully wondering if I would ever attain to the place where God could trust me with His counsels in this way. I did not know that God has these gifts in greater or less measure for all who are born again of the Spirit and living in obedience to that Holy Spirit. I was soon to learn.

Joy at Father's recovery was quickly followed by a new anxiety. Mother had been the business head in the family. It was she who had managed to make ends meet and who had planned so carefully that I was able to get an education. Father was of Micawber's optimistic and gullible temperament. He was always going to "strike it rich" by investment in copper, silver, or gold mines, or some such venture. The fact that he had consistently lost all his life savings in these "promising" stocks never seemed to teach him. After Mother's death I was perturbed to hear that Father had given up his profession and had gone in for stock selling, this time a new invention which would make us all millionaires in a short time! Brother, too, had sold his chicken ranch and apparently was not working at anything. Why start something new if you are going to be independently wealthy soon? They rented a little bungalow in North Vancouver, sold some of our furniture, and moved the rest in. These cheerful, wonderful-sounding letters only served to burden me. The higher Daddy's expectations rose, the lower sank my heart!

"Lord, is life to be always grim?" I whispered to Him. His answer was not long in coming.

It was in General Missions class that Dr. Glover repeated a previous announcement. "I have told you before," he said, "of the Foreign Missions Convention of the United States and Canada to be held in Washington, DC, January 28 to February 2. The Moody Bible Institute has been allotted eight delegates, but we only have six signed up to go. This will be a wonderful experience, since famous missionaries and native converts from all over the world are coming. President Coolidge is to open the session. I am sure there are some in the student body who can afford to pay their own way. The time is getting short. I would urge you to sign up. Next week is the last opportunity, so get ready."

Delegate to a great missionary conference in the nation's capital! My heart reached out in longing to go. Suddenly I felt I was to go. It was as if the Lord said, "You had a long enough siege of sorrow, dear. I'm going to send you to Washington for a little time of joy."

I thrilled through and through and believed Him. Yet it was an impossible hope. I had not a cent to put toward the expense. All week long I imagined the Lord sending me a huge gift of money and my trotting up to Dr. Glover and offering to be a delegate — but not a cent came in.

The last day of opportunity arrived. At Missions class that morning several student volunteers had been asked to speak three minutes each, telling why they felt they should go to the foreign field. At the end, Dr. Glover again made an impassioned plea for one more delegate to the Washington conference. The opportunity would close that night, he said. I left the class wondering if it had been the voice of the Lord I heard, or had I been deceived by wishful thinking? That noon there was a note in my mailbox. Call at Dr. Glover's office immediately, it read. With high-bounding heart I ran to the building where the Director of Missions had his office. Trembling with excitement, I knocked at the door.

"Come in! . . . Oh, Miss Miller, sit down." Dr. Glover beamed at me. "I sent for you to tell you that someone has offered to pay your way to the conference. Would you like to go?"

"Oh," I gasped. "Would I? But who could the donor be?" I wondered if perhaps Dr. and Mrs. Page might have offered this help, but how could they afford it?

"The donor wishes to remain unknown," Dr. Glover replied, "and I believe she is a stranger to you." He had said she, so I knew it was a woman! He went on. "She has paid your fare, your hotel fees, and meals, and has added an extra twenty dollars just for fun. Here it is. The rail fare and hotel bill I'll pay for you. Now you'll have to be ready to leave by tomorrow. Can you make it? I already have permission for you from the Dean of Women."

I made it, all right!

But I would like to tell you how God worked this out for me. The dear benefactress did allow me to know the story later on. She was a well-to-do Christian, recently widowed. That Thursday morning she happened to be downtown on business near the institute. Glancing at her watch, she saw there was time to slip in and listen to Dr. Glover's Mission Hour. As she slipped into a seat among the students, I was called up to give my testimony. When I had finished, Mrs. X– whispered to the girl seated next to her, "Who was that speaker?"

We neither of us knew who that girl was, but she told not only my name but also added, "Isobel has been going through deep sorrow. Her mother died before Christmas and a few weeks later her father was nearly killed in an accident." The kind little widow's heart went out to me, her own bereavement still fresh upon her. So when Dr. Glover arose to make a last plea for the one remaining delegate, she felt instantly that she would like to send me. A change of scene, inspiring messages, sightseeing around the capital, she thought, is just what that girl needs. I'll give it to her, and incidentally Moody Bible Institute can have its full quota of delegates.

God bless His generous stewards who live in the flow of His thoughts so that He can think and act through them.

Such spiritual premonitions I never had before I found the Lord. From time to time I have had them ever since. I believe they are given for the purpose of comfort and to refresh our experience that He is there, and that He cares. Only God could have worked out that little forecast and fulfillment.

So began one of the high peaks of joy which tower up exultantly above the painful valley experiences of my life. It was one that has always been outstanding. It molded my life as I little suspected it would have any power to do, for one of the other eight delegates was John B. Kuhn.

I had been formally introduced to him at last, and it was at a mixed party after all! The occasion was Daddy Page's birthday. A group of young Student Volunteers whom the Pages had often had at their home decided to give him a surprise party. I was told there would be boys present and also that one of these would be the brother of Kathryn Kuhn, so I knew I was to meet him at last.

How could I get out of it? If it had been the birthday of a member of the staff, for instance, I could have found an excuse. But my own dear Daddy Page — I just had to go to his birthday party!

The group was to meet at half past seven on the corner of Clark Street, where we caught the street car. We girls arrived first. The moon was rising over the tall old houses when we saw the group of boys approaching. "Oh, here they come!" cried the leader of us girls. "Miss Miller, let me introduce Jack Graham and John Kuhn and —" I heard no more. I found myself looking straight into the face of the dishwasher from the Bible Institute kitchen!

It was a wonderful convention, with world-renowned missionaries taking part. We heard them speak and met some of them personally. Between meetings we went sightseeing. We visited the White House and were presented to President Coolidge, shaking hands with him. After it was over we all had a short trip to Mount Vernon to see the home of George and Martha Washington. What good times we had — sitting together, eating together, sightseeing through snow-slushy Washington, laughing and teasing when we set out to buy Gordon Hedderly Smith some rubbers, only to hear the clerk say they did not carry such a large size!

How little we knew of what future years would hold. That two of the delegates would marry each other and serve Him in far off Lisuland. That Jack Graham would serve in the same province, ministering to the Miao tribe. That Irene Forsythe would have a wonderful ministry in Shantung among the Chinese. That Gordon Smith would open up work among many new tribes in Indochina. Friendships were formed during those delegate days that have sweetened the whole road of life ever since.

CHAPTER TEN
AT SUNDRY TIMES AND IN DIVERS MANNERS

When is The Search ended? In one sense, it is finished when our hand, stretched out to God in the name of His appointed mediator Jesus Christ feels the answering grasp and knows that He is there. But in another sense the searching never ends. The first discovery is quickly followed by another, and that by another. And so it goes on.

As I write it is dawning a new day. The far horizon saw the bright spot of the rising sun, but heavy clouds soon covered it. These clouds have become illuminated. Streaks of pink and gold beauty break through chance rents in their filmy cover. Glory after glory appears as the eye eagerly explores the heavens.

So it is with God. To find that He is, this is the mere starting point of our search. We are lured on to explore what He is, and that search is never finished. It grows more thrilling the further one proceeds.

Up to this point I have discovered that God is, and that He is mine by mediatorship of Christ. I have discovered that He can and will teach me His way or His plan for my life. I have found that He can overcome obstacles and that we do not need to arouse a great hullabaloo to get Him to do so. Hudson Taylor was right in his discovery: "Learn to move man through God by prayer alone." By searching I have discovered that God has strange and sweet ways of manifesting Himself. At sundry times and in divers manners He is still speaking.

He is just as versatile in caring for the needs of those who trust Him, and in this chapter I am going to tell how He provided for me in different ways at different times. I have already told how, through Marjorie Harrison, God provided my fare to Chicago, and board and room at the institute for one year. I have also told of His remarkable provision for my trip to Washington. How He made provision for the autumn term of 1925, when Marjorie's money had all been used up and I was entirely dependent on my own earnings is another story of God's care. It involves another life which had touched mine the previous spring.

It must have been about April, 1925, that I was struck by a prayer request given in the evening devotions hours. A graduate student got up and asked prayer for "a girlfriend who has suffered a terrible tragedy and lost her faith. She is coming to see me at the institute. Pray she may find the Lord again."

A girl struck by heartbreak pushed onto The Misty Flats and floundering bitterly. I saw it all with a sympathy that pierced my heart. *Lord, give her to me*, I prayed inwardly. *Oh, I can understand how she feels!* I felt He answered that He would.

Humanly speaking, there was no likelihood of our meeting in the ordinary course of events. I was now working part time as a noon rush-hour waitress. The graduate student who had given the request moved in a different circle. "The elite" we laughingly dubbed those students who were wealthy enough to go through school without working their way. They had plenty of leisure, and we had none, so "the elite" and "the workers" seldom met outside of classrooms. They had picnics and parties for which we could not afford the time. Naturally each group clanned together.

I could have pushed my way up to the graduate student and asked for an introduction and would have been nicely received. But I decided that if it were of the Lord, He must work it out in His own way. Then I would know that it was not my own impulsive wishing. I prayed about it.

The strange thing is that neither Ruth nor I can remember how it came about. I have a dim recollection of a chance encounter in the post office. I was watching the elite set for the appearance of a stranger, so spotted her early. She was tall and slim, with naturally curly light brown hair, and the soft accent of a Southerner. Why she noticed me among the hundreds of unfamiliar girl faces at the institute, I will never know. God answered my prayer and "gave" me Ruth. That is all I need to say.

Soon she was coming to our room for talks and pursuing me wherever she could catch this student laborer. I remember once encountering her just before the noon hour, when I was rushing off to be waitress at that restaurant, the employees' restaurant of a large corporation nearby.

"I want to talk to you!" she said.

"Fine," I answered. "Can you come in tonight? I'm on my way to work now and dare not stop. I'll just barely make it."

"No!" she replied petulantly. "I want to talk now. I'll walk with you to your job. Nothing against that, is there ma'am?" (We had great fun over the difference in Canadian and Southern speech forms. To me, ma'am was the language of a servant to a mistress; to her it was the polite way to apologize. She laughed much and mimicked drolly my *I beg your pardon?* and rubbed in her *ma'am* as often as possible with a teasing sparkle in her eyes.)

I was just a little diffident about Ruth seeing me in that restaurant. I was servant to the servants there, so to speak, and the rush-hour girls had to take left-over apron uniforms, usually very ill-fitting ones. Ruth was the only child of well-to-do people. Cultured homes were her natural environment. What would she say if she saw me in that restaurant?

She was quick to notice my slight hesitation in accepting her escort, and nothing would shake her off from that moment. Right into the restaurant she came and saw it all — saw, too, my embarrassment, and mischievously determined to make the most of it.

Ruth was the twentieth-century counterpart of Mary Tudor, sister of Henry VIII. Charming, capricious, affectionate, and utterly lovable; clever and nimble-witted, she was still untamed. To use a more vulgar but more explicit word, she was unspanked. Her parents had spared the rod, and that kind of upbringing always follows a child through the rest of life.

It was impossible ever to "handle" Ruth. She saw you tuck the handle under your apron just as soon as you moved your arm, and with an almost devilish mischief she would whisk it out and brandish it before your chagrined face and defy you. She was my superior in personality, brains, social culture — in everything but one thing. She did not possess the fellowship of the Lord Jesus Christ or know Him as I did. That was what I longed that she might have. But I had not been with her long before I knew I could never "deal" with her. She was too quick to recognize any such effort, and she had my own resentment at the invasion of her spiritual sanctum. She would open it up when and where she liked, but no one should knock it open. The only thing I knew to do was to love her and pray for her.

Somewhere along the line, maybe in an evening session, relaxed on her bed, talking in the dark, she suddenly opened up and told me her tragedy. She had become engaged to one of God's finest gentlemen, one who knew Him and served Him devoutly. But they had quarreled, and Ruth had highhandedly broken their engagement. She had never really meant to break with Jack; she loved him too dearly for that. But she had conceived a pique against life for disappointing her, and had to take it out on someone. At the first overture Jack might make, she would melt and be his own darling Ruth again — that was her inward thought. But no overture came. She did not know that even while she had this tiff with him, he was going down with a fever. When she did learn of it, he was already in heaven.

After this she had an unfortunate experience with a religious hypocrite. With her lightning-like petulance, she had said she could not believe in God when a Christian would act like that.

Yes, it is better to have the rod when you are a child. When life must wield it against you, it is too cruel. Can you think what her agonies were? Not just to have lost him — their wedding date had been set — but to have him go before she was able to say, "Oh, I did not mean it! I'm sorry. Please forgive me."

Her kind, worldly father did the best he knew. He handed her his check book and said, "Go to New York and have a good time. Forget the irrevocable."

She went, and all the wild life she led I did not care to hear about. One question was making my heart stand still: "Ruth, did you not grope for the low road?"

She was silent for a moment. "I know what you mean. No. Somehow there has always been in me a hidden passion for chastity. But I did everything else — I was wild."

I sighed a *thank God!* Christ can save from the low road, where man "wallows in fleshly things until his appetites become fibrous," as, praise God, our city rescue missions all testify. As for the hidden passion for chastity, I understood that too.

Hast thou heard Him, seen Him, known Him?
Is not thine a captured heart?

Anyone who has ever really known the Lord, even only in reflection, can never again be satisfied with less.

"Did the check book and New York's wildest help?" I asked.

She withered me with a look. "You know it didn't."

How I prayed for this dear, honest, if willful young life. I thought I had been able to help her out from The Misty Flats, but later she was sucked back in again. She is His now, however. In my Moody autograph book, a large tome, her autograph covers four pages, written in three installments. The first is one of her nonsense poems, shrewd with perspicuity. (She has a literary gift, among other things. The elite publishing houses reach after her manuscripts! They do not even know that I exist.)

The third installment reads:

Wonder if I'll ever finish this — sounds like *The Perils of Ruth* in three installments. What I've been trying to say for the last two pages is that I love you (just plain, unadulterated, simple-minded love). You have meant so very much to me — you, yourself — and you have meant infinitely more in that you have both showed me the way and fought with me during these hard days of decision. I can wish no greater thing than that you may mean just that to these dear folks in China.

I know that Ruth had been "sifting" me. When she caught a glimpse of pride wincing, she seized on it and walked right to the restaurant to see every bit of it. More than that, at a later date, without any warning she brought a college girlfriend with her to that same restaurant to catch me as I was.

But she did more than sift. Tenderly affectionate and generous, she discovered that I enjoyed beautiful things. Maybe it began by her getting permission from the dean to take me out for a meal, so we would have more time to talk. My frank delight in the harmonious drapes, shaded lights, and soft classical dinner music amused Ruth. From then on she deliberately hunted up quaint, pretty tearooms and increased the frequency of her invitations. With her unfailing charm, she could wangle a permission out of a dean that no one else would even dare to propose. And so she "embroidered" my days.

But her careless use of money shocked me. When away from Chicago she once sent me a telegram in lieu of a letter. When I remonstrated by letter I received a second telegram to laugh at me! No, you could not "handle" Ruth!

There came a day, however, when, to her astonishment, she found that someone else could be hard to handle too. The summer of 1925 I spent in Canada with my Aunt Nellie, Mother's younger sister. On returning to the institute I now faced having to support myself entirely. This meant working three times a day instead of only at noon, but I was highly favored. I had obtained the post of waitress at the faculty table in the institute dining room. This meant being down half an hour before each meal to prepare the food nicely. It also meant staying half an hour afterward to wash up and set the table. In addition there was the time consumed in having my meal after the other students had already finished theirs. It was not too strenuous, however, for it was work among Christians; no more heathen Americans shouting at me. It was exacting, for I had to be there right on time, but it was no great distance away as the other job had been. No time was wasted in getting to work.

One day I was in the act of preparing a meal when in breezed Ruth. She had arrived unexpectedly with her parents for a short visit. "So this is where we are now!" she teased. "Say, I've got something to tell you."

With an eye on the clock hand which was traveling close toward my deadline, I said, Keep it, dearie, until tonight — can you? I'm dying to hear it, but my job has to come first. I have to get this finished before the faculty arrives. I'm working full-time this term." There would be no more meals out in pretty tearooms.

Ruth stood and pouted. "But I want to talk to you about my soul!" she said with a twinkle in her eye. "How important is that? And you stand there flaying radishes into rosebuds and say, 'Another time.' How do you know I'll feel like talking about it at another time? There is something wrong here. Something's got to be done about this."

Then she had to leave because the faculty had begun to arrive.

I felt very uncomfortable. It was true that Ruth wasn't the kind of person who could open up the doors of her sanctum at any odd moment. On the other hand, I had to work. Surely the Lord expected faithfulness in my job. Inwardly I prayed for help and went on with the task in hand.

Ruth was busy too. She arrived in my room that evening her old gay self. "I have it all arranged!" she said happily. "No more table serving for Little Pats!"

That was her pet name for me. Apparently I am addicted to short, quick movements when showing affection — many short, little kisses, and many little pats on the back in a hug. My children laugh at the former and Ruth declared she got homesick for the latter. The name has pursued me through the years.

"I told my father about you," Ruth continued. "He says he will be delighted to support you through the rest of your schooling here. Now then! Whenever Ruthie arrives and needs talking to, she can have it. And many others too. Don't you see the Lord's hand in this, ma'am?" — with roguish delight.

But I didn't, and there was an awkward silence. Ruth's father was a fine, clean man, but he played the races and gained his money in the usual worldly ways. Hudson Taylor believed firmly that God does not need, and will not use for blessing, money offered by unbelievers. God is able to provide for His own children apart from help from those who serve mammon. "We can afford to have as little as the Lord chooses to give," he once said, "but we cannot afford to have unconsecrated money." But would Ruth ever be able to understand what I meant by refusing on that score? Her eyes sparkled with mischievous delight when I said her father's money was unconsecrated. She would have a good time telling him that! Miserably, I tried to explain without appearing ungrateful. But when she saw that it really touched what was sacred to me, she accepted it quietly, for Ruth was a lady born. When her visit ended I was still faculty waitress.

But I had not counted on Ruth's decisiveness. After a week or so, I received a letter from her. I wish I had it by me to quote from now, for nothing reveals her charm as much as her little notes. It simply stated that she had got herself a job teaching physical culture at their local YWCA, and her monthly salary was enough to pay my room and board. Now, she wanted to know, was that consecrated enough for me to use, ma'am? Not one cent of her father's money would taint it. "Now, Lambkins, you know it will be good for Ruth to have to hold down a job! Now don't you? Just think of the good you are doing me by accepting and thus making me an honest worker in the hive of life, and not a drone. Please write and tell me you accept."

So Ruth had "handled" me after all. I was never able to handle her, but that is how the Lord sent me support for the closing school term of 1925.

For Christmas, 1925, I was invited to the Harrison home. Dr. and Mrs. Norman B. Harrison were now living in St. Louis where he was pastor of the famous old Washington-Compton Presbyterian Church. They have a family of six talented children, and with two or three of us guests added we made an hilarious house party. Members of his congregation invited us out to meals and helped to entertain us, but the most fun were the good times in their own home, where music and youthful antics embellished every day.

I arrived back at the institute in January, 1926, expecting to continue in my luxurious leisure. A letter from Ruth awaited me.

She had taken sick and the doctor forbade her to continue with her physical culture class. "Please let Father support you until I get stronger," she wailed. But I could not consider it; it was not the pattern God had showed me. One of my lodestar verses was Hebrews 8:5: "See . . . that thou make all things according to the pattern shewed to thee in the mount."

From the mountaintop to the valley in one swing. How often life does just that! One moment having all things and at the peak of fun, the next moment facing a grim poverty and hard work. I had to seek employment now. I had lost the comfortable faculty waitress job and it was never available for me again.

Totally unprepared for this, I had not been careful in my spending, and I now anxiously marshaled out my funds. There was just enough to pay the first month's board — we paid in advance — with something like eleven or twelve dollars over. I would barely make it. I must go to the employment office immediately and see what jobs they could find me. The nicer jobs would all be gone by this time. More than that, friends had been told I was being supported all through school and no one would think to send me any extra gifts. But the Lord had not left me. It was another chance to search His powers. He was asking me to be willing for uncongenial work again.

As I sat looking at my accounts I suddenly saw something that made me go cold. In the Christmas rush I had forgotten to tithe my last income. What should I do? Let the tithe continue to slide for a while? I pondered a moment. What came first in life anyway? "Oh, Lord, You come first," I whispered and resolutely set aside the tithe. That left me less than two dollars for a months' carfare and incidentals. And I still had no job.

The institute's employment bureau found me two jobs: noon rush-hour girl at the same old restaurant, and waitress for evening school supper at the institute. I was now very busy indeed. The long walk to and from the restaurant, and a later hour getting to bed from the evening school began to tell on my health. Always thin, it was dangerous for me to lose weight, but I knew I was doing so. By February my friends were beginning to notice that I looked haggard and tired. I myself felt I was near the breaking point. "Lord, is it Thy will that I have a breakdown?" I prayed in private.

One evening I was called over to the reception room to meet a visitor. Standing there, tall, smiling, and fatherly, was Dr. Harrison. In the city on special speaking engagements, he thought he would look me up.

His keen eyes searched me as we shook hands. "How is it, Isobel?" he asked. "You look tired. Not working too hard, are you?"

"Perhaps I am," I answered. "When I returned here from your place I found that I must work my way again. The lady who had been supporting me since Marjorie stopped has been sick and cannot do it any more."

"Well, Isobel"— and the keen, kindly eyes again searched my face — "isn't it wonderful that *stop* isn't in the Lord's vocabulary? He never gets sick, He never forgets our needs, and He is never at the end of His resources. Do you remember when you were at our place at Christmas that you were invited out to dinner with Marjorie by a Miss Boyle?"

Oh, yes, that had been a real treat. Miss Boyle was a wealthy lady in Dr. Harrison's congregation. She lived in an exclusive apartment hotel, the kind of place where an ordinary mortal scarcely dared to look, much less enter. Because of her love for Marjorie, Miss Boyle had included me in the invitation, but she had scarcely noticed me beyond the usual courteous care of one's guests. I had not minded. It left me free to enjoy the exquisite appointments of the room, the table, and the meal. How much the Lord did give me! "As having nothing and yet possessing all things." I was beginning to understand what Paul meant. But Dr. Harrison was talking.

"I saw Miss Boyle just before I left. When she heard me say I was coming to speak at the institute, she said, 'By the way, I was thinking the other day that I have never made any gifts directly to a student at Moody Bible Institute. I feel I would like to help that little friend of Marjorie's who came to my place for lunch that day.' And Isobel, she handed me a check for two hundred dollars. I intended to give it you in small gifts, perhaps ten dollars at a time, but maybe I'd better give it all to you now."

Two hundred dollars — just like that. Truly *at sundry times and in divers manners.*

"Oh, if you did," I cried, "then I could give up one of my jobs and not have to work so hard."

"I'll see you get it tomorrow, dear," said the dear servant of the Lord, who went on his way.

So I was able to give up the evening work. The noon rush hour, though disagreeable, paid better for the time used, so I retained it. By this and with other gifts I managed to pay my way until summer.

When I returned for the last term, September through December, 1926, I was once more faced with earning my way entirely. The employment bureau put me in touch with Mrs. Frances Allison of the Practical Work Department. She gave me a very special assignment for Sundays, one which paid a salary! I was the Sunday pianist for St. Charles Reformatory for Boys, with the government paying the bill. I gasped at the assignment and expostulated to Mrs. Allison, "Oh, I can't play the piano well enough to hold down that job! I am largely self taught. Always before, this assignment has been given to a music major student. Isn't that so?"

"True," Mrs. Allison answered, "but I have heard you play for evening devotions, and I think you can make it. I'll ask one of our instructors to give you some tips on evangelistic piano playing and get permission for you to practice on one of the pianos in the music department. The reason I chose you is that the assignment gives such a wonderful opportunity for personal work, and the lady who has been in charge until now is sick. The friend substituting for her is quite inexperienced in bringing children to decisions. You know the reformatory, don't you? Every kind of boy problem is there, from playing hooky from school to murder.

There have been some remarkable conversions and we don't want to see it slump. You are paid to play for the morning and afternoon services, but are allowed to visit the boys who are sick in the infirmary and deal personally with them between services. You get two meals into the bargain, so it will help you financially."

With fear and trembling I accepted, and for four months, every Sunday brought me thrilling experiences. "My strength encampeth on weakness" is one rendering of II Corinthians 12:9. The substitute leader who taught the Sunday school lesson in the morning service was very conscious of her inexperience, and the pianist trembled lest she be called on to give a piano solo, which sometimes happened. Truly I was weak. Therefore the Lord alone was exalted when scores of those boys decided for Christ. I could fill a chapter with all that took place at St. Charles Reformatory, but this is a chapter on finances, so I must continue with that theme.

Of course, the salary for piano playing was only a mite. I had to take a major job besides that. The employment office found me another job as a waitress since those hours fitted my schedule best. But it was at a select tearoom near Michigan Boulevard. Noon and evening I was to serve, and the salary promised was good. It was situated in a private house, and the clientele were mostly high-salaried clerks or office workers from the wealthy district around. Undoubtedly I would get good tips in addition to the good salary. The widowed proprietor, Mrs. Mac, had been investigated, the moral atmosphere of the place approved, and all was trustworthy. Now at last I ought to have plenty of money. This was a good thing, for the last term of school always brings extra expenses.

I liked it very much. Mrs. Mac was a middle-aged southern lady, gracious and warmhearted. The tearoom was pretty, the food delicious, and the clientele very nice to me. My tips grew, and I was congratulating myself when a cloud appeared. At the end of the first month I walked in one morning to hear shouts and high words. The cook was swearing at Mrs. Mac, who was at the telephone.

"Isobel, stay here in this room," commanded Mrs. Mac, all flushed up. "This woman is threatening my life. I've called the police and I do not dare to be left alone with her until they come here and put her out."

"No need for the police if you will give me my salary!" shouted the excited and irate cook. "This is a place for you to be in, Miss Isobel! She pays nobody! I've worked here two months and have been paid hardly anything. She owes the butcher, the baker, the—"

"Shut up!" cried Mrs. Mac. "You lie." And they were at it again when a tall policeman arrived at the door and the cook had to leave.

My heart sank. That wonderful salary would I really get it? It was the end of the month and payday. Just what was the situation, anyhow? Within half an hour a new cook had arrived, and the business of the day rushed on, but as I went from table to table, my mind was busy on this problem. Should I ask Mrs. Mac for my salary? Or should I just pray that God would move her to give it to me?

By the end of the day I had made a decision. I would speak if she did not offer to settle accounts. She made no offer, nor did she give any hint that she remembered my salary was due.

"Mrs. Mac," I said as I put on my hat and coat, "tomorrow is the first of the month, and I must pay my board and room bill at the institute. Do you think you could let me have my salary tonight?"

She hesitated, then went slowly over to the till. "I had an unexpectedly big bill to pay today," she said.

"Could you take half your salary now, and I'll pay you the rest later?"

This was what I had feared. The dismissed cook had told the truth. Mrs. Mac was not in the habit of paying her bills. Her promises were wonderful, but it was quite a different thing to get her to keep them. Again I was in a predicament. If I reported this to the institute, they would recall me, of course. But at this late date what other jobs would be available? Here at least I received something from tips. In fact, my tips for the first month, combined with what she had just given me, almost equaled the sum of the promised salary. This gave me an idea.

"Mrs. Mac," I said earnestly, "I am a Christian and accustomed to asking God directly for what I need. I cannot serve you for nothing, but I am willing to keep track of my tips, and at the end of each week if you will make up what is lacking to the amount you promised to pay, I will be content with that. Then we will ask the Lord to move the clients to tip me as much as is needed."

She flushed a little. 'But that is not right, Isobel," she said. "The tips should be yours as extra."

"But I am content and can make ends meet if I get what you originally promised me," I replied.

"It is very good of you," she said sadly, then opened up and told me her troubles. She was utterly undisciplined and improvident, having no conscience about debt, and spent freely what came into the till.

Each Saturday I faithfully reported my tips, which continued to be high. Better able to part with a small sum than a large one, Mrs. Mac gave me her portion. I believe now that I was the only worker she hired who got paid regularly. Of course I talked to her about trusting the Lord for salvation. She liked to listen and often agreed with me, but as far as I could see, the miracle of a new birth within her never took place. I fear the habit of dishonest thinking had become her refuge from conscience. The new cook lasted only six or eight weeks, and then there was a scene similar to the first one. She would pay a little on her big butcher's and grocery bills, just enough to keep the stores from suing her. But of course that way of doing business could not go on forever.

One December morning I walked in to find the tearoom empty — nothing cooking in the kitchen, and nothing prepared for the lunch-hour clientele. I called Mrs. Mac, but there was no answer.

The upper stories of this beautiful old home had been let out to roomers. One of them, hearing me, came downstairs, dressed for departure. "There has been a big blowup here," she said in a low voice. "I didn't get it all, but I think the old lady has gone bankrupt. The cook made a furor about salary not paid, and Mrs. Mac said she wished she were dead. Do you think she can have hung herself in the cellar? Better go down and have a look! I'm going to my office. Goodbye." And I was left alone in the empty room.

A nerve-racking experience followed. All was silent as the grave, and my imagination conjured up an image of going down in a cellar and bumping into her dead body dangling from the rafters. I shook all over and couldn't get up enough courage to open that cellar door. I prayed for the courage to go down and look, but did not receive it. I despised myself and lectured myself and asked the Lord how I could ever go to China if I did not have nerve enough to open a cellar door and go down to investigate. But I was petrified. I just could not do it.

After about an hour I heard a step on the veranda and ran forward to see another live human being. It was Mrs. Mac.

"Oh, Isobel," she said with a heavy sigh. "I forgot

113

about you. There won't be any more tearoom. I'm bankrupt, and the receivers are coming to take over the building. I've lost everything. I couldn't stand the silence, so I've been out for a walk."

"Mrs. Mac, I do wish you would give yourself to the Lord!" I said, trying again to help her. But nothing seemed to penetrate her mind. She was appreciative, almost affectionate toward me, but in spiritual matters she was vacant. She would not acknowledge she was a sinner, and that is the first step toward knowing God, so I had to leave her.

Again I was in a predicament. Only a few weeks until graduation and no income! I remember only two details of those last days. Mother had left me her silver service and Father asked to buy it from me for fifty dollars. That helped a lot.

Then came a day when a bill was due and I was five dollars short. I had been praying about it, but nothing had come in. The morning I had to pay it, I received a letter in which five dollars was enclosed. It was a letter from an old Christian lady whom my father had visited. When he told her I was working my way through Moody, she decided to send me that gift. She had not given me anything before, and she never gave me anything afterward, but on the morning of my lack her five dollars arrived.

At sundry times and in divers manners, always the good hand of my God was upon me. He had wrought wonderfully for Hudson Taylor, but as I looked back over my two years and four months at the Moody Bible Institute I felt He had done just as wonderful things for this little, unknown Bible student. *By searching* I had found God able and faithful to supply my financial needs. And He will do this for any of His children who trust and obey Him.

CHAPTER ELEVEN

GRADUATION AND CIM CANDIDATURE

I was elected girl class speaker for the graduation exercises in December, 1926. I prayed for a message, taking as my theme, The Print of the Nails, based on Thomas's words in John 20:25, "Except I shall see in his hands the print of the nails, and put my finger into the print of the nails, and thrust my hand into his side, I will not believe." I made it representative of what the unbelieving world is unconsciously saying to the Christian church today. The unbelievers around us have not much respect or interest in a smug, ordinary Christianity. "If it costs you nothing, what proof have you that it has any value?" is their indifferent, shrugging attitude. But when they see in any life the print of the nails, they are challenged, and, like Thomas of old, if they can be made to see Him at that moment, they will fall down and cry, "My Lord and my God!"

I felt this message deeply and wanted it to speak to other hearts as it had to my own. The valedictory messages had to be written out, checked for doctrine and grammar, and be memorized by the speakers. This bothered me a little. I didn't mind memorizing the speech, but I had never been able to pour out my heart unless given the freedom of extemporaneous speaking. I did not know this at the time, for I had done comparatively little public speaking. All I knew was that I felt hampered, somehow, on reciting a memorized text. But rules were rules, and I fell in line, as I had tried to do throughout my school days.

My father came to Chicago for my graduation, and Miss Boyle sent me a white silk dress. She and I did not correspond. In fact, apart from the two-hundred-dollar gift at the beginning of that year, I had heard nothing from her. Certainly no one was told I had no money to buy the required white dress for graduation! Remember, I had lost my employment at Mrs. Mac's.

Moreover, in those days, Moody Bible Institute required that girl students' clothing have sleeves below the elbow and skirts nine inches from the floor. The 1926 styles were worn shorter than that, yet when Miss Ruby Jackson, registrar of the faculty, measured the gift dress, it fulfilled all the requirements and did not have to be altered at all!

Miss Boyle's gifts to me ended here. I have never heard from her since.

As we went up to the platform, on sudden impulse I gave the text of my message to Anne Barr, our vice president, just in case I got stage fright and needed prompting. I had recited the whole thing more than once before our speech instructor, so it was not that I did not know it.

When my name was called, I went forward and faced that big audience. I did not feel as nervous as I expected to, and started in easily. But as I proceeded, I felt that I was merely reciting and not pouring out my soul. I felt the message was not going into the hearts of the audience. In my anxiety to give it the meaning it had for me, I forgot how the next paragraph started. Only for a second, however. Behind me, Anne prompted quickly in a low voice that not everybody heard, but to me it was a catastrophe. I got through the message, went to my seat, hung my head, and waited until the end of the program when I would be free to dash for my room. During my last term I had a room to myself. Once up there I fell on my knees in an agony of humiliation and failure.

Through the heavy city atmosphere, a pale December sun shone weakly on me. Then suddenly the Lord was there in the room. I felt His love folding me around. "Never mind, dear," He was saying. "Failure or success, it is all over now, and My love is just the same."

"The beloved of the Lord shall dwell in safety by him and the Lord shall cover him all the day long, and he shall dwell between his shoulders" (Deut. 33:12).

The words came to me as if spoken, and the tenderness that engulfed me was as the balm of Gilead to my agonized soul. Slowly I quieted, relaxed, rested back on Him, and drank deeply of His love. It was a wonderful experience and I was lifted up in spirit so that I no longer cared about any personal humiliation. I was deeply sorry to have disappointed the expectation of my class, but apart from that I was beyond hurt. I have never forgotten the outpouring of God's love upon me that day when I felt such a failure.

After graduation came candidature at the China Inland Mission in Toronto. The 1926 candidates class had been held in August. Kathryn Kuhn and her brother John, with many others, had been accepted. The party sailed for China in October. I was the only candidate applying in midwinter. As I would be leaving for my home on the Pacific coast, the mission decided that I should come to Toronto immediately after graduation. Toronto being the place of my birth, we had relatives and friends there with whom my father stayed, waiting until he and I could travel west together.

Daddy Page came to the train to see us off. I do not

know whether I was looking anxious or sad or just plain tired, but suddenly a tender compassion lit up his face. He leaned forward. "Don't be afraid, Isobel," he said. "There is nothing to dread in candidate school. The CIM has known you from a child."

I thanked him for this good cheer and for all his loving, fatherly care of me during my institute days. Then the train pulled out.

The Rev. and Mrs. E. A. Brownlee were in charge of the Toronto Mission Home. But Mr. Roy Seaman was the one appointed to start me on Chinese language study. The Seamans were on furlough and staying at the home. Candidates learn to recognize the difficult radicals, which roughly correspond to the English alphabet, and other simple beginnings. I was also to help and act as companion to the widow of one of the mission's donors whose bereavement had made her distraught. Her family felt the quiet, prayerful atmosphere of the CIM home might benefit her.

Dana, son of Mr. and Mrs. Brownlee, lived in the home. The only other young person I remember was Miss Ida McInnes. I had met Ida at Moody. She had organized Daddy Page's surprise birthday party and had introduced me to John, and I had learned to love her. She had graduated earlier and applied to the China Inland Mission but did not pass the medical examination. With China closed to her, she became the office worker for the Mission to Lepers, but was allowed to stay on in the CIM home until she could find a boardinghouse elsewhere.

Ida was "the embroidery" to my candidate days. She was devoted to the Lord, and we were one in the things of the Spirit. Her keen sense of humor was a safety valve for my youthful spirits. Quick, impulsive, and daydreaming, I had been an easy prey to faux pas all my life. I was not in the home twenty-four hours before I made the first one.

Knowing the Brownlees' reputation for perfect administration, I am sure the fault was mine, but I did not know the daily schedule. Most likely they had told me while I was daydreaming! Conscious that this was more than probable, I felt shy to ask what the hours were, and decided to watch carefully the bells which summoned the household to meals and meetings. I got along well the first morning, but at half-past one in the afternoon I was startled by the clang of a bell. What did that call me to? I rushed to Ida's room, but she was out. A girl was dusting in the corridor, so I asked her, "What was the bell for, please?"

She looked at me wonderingly and announced, "It's the prayer meeting bell."

A prayer meeting? And the candidate not attending? That would look bad!

"Sorry," I said hastily. "I'm new here. Which room is it?"

She told me, indicating the office buildings, and I rushed over. The door was shut, but a murmur of voices within settled it for me. I knocked gently and opened it. In my excitement, I did not notice that only the staff were present!

"Excuse me for being late," I murmured and sank into a seat.

They received me politely, albeit a little blankly, and that day the staff prayers were very general! After the meeting, Mrs. Brownlee came and told me gently that the half-past one meeting was for the staff only and that my presence would not be required.

How Ida laughed when I told her! "They probably discuss you at that meeting!" she teased. From then on there were many pointed remarks as to when my presence was required and when it wasn't. We had hilarious times in her room.

I was in Toronto some three or four weeks before being called to meet the council. That is a formidable occasion, and I was nervous, as I am not quick at thinking on my feet. I always do better with preparation and time to consider the best answer. The meeting came and went, however. That evening after supper, I was called into the sitting room by Mr. Brownlee to hear the verdict. He said something like this: "The council was quite satisfied with your answers today, and we in the home have enjoyed your presence. But the council has asked me to speak to you upon a very serious matter. Among your references there was one who did not recommend you. The reason given was that you are proud, disobedient, and likely to be a troublemaker. This person has known you for some years, and the council felt they could not ignore the criticism."

"Who was it?" I asked quickly, simply dumfounded.

"The CIM does not betray the confidence of references. We write to those who have had business associations with you as well as the references you yourself give. And we promise to keep all reports in confidence. I cannot tell you the name, but I would like to discuss with you what havoc such characteristics can cause on the field."

He then proceeded to do so. At the end of an hour of earnest exhortation, he pronounced the verdict. "The council decided to accept you conditionally. There is an anti-foreign uprising in China just now which is very serious, and we dare not send out any new candidates. That will be our public statement on this matter.

"For yourself alone, and we hope you will not spread it around, during your waiting period the Vancouver Council will be watching to see if any of these characteristics show themselves. If you prove that you have conquered them, you will then meet with the Western Council and be accepted fully and sent out with the first party that goes. As we anticipate your victory in these matters, it was voted to pay your train fare to Vancouver as en route for China.

"I can assure you I have not found it easy to say these things." Indeed, his face was sad and tired. I felt sorry for him, even with the misery that was numbing my own heart.

I went up to bed, but as you can readily believe, not to sleep. Who could be the unknown referee?

Proud. Disobedient. A troublemaker. This was the third time the adjective proud had been attached to me. The first time was by Daddy Page months before. He had read me an anxious lecture on the subject, to my extreme surprise. Pride was one of the human frailties of which I felt I was not guilty. I would have taken Daddy Page's lecture to heart if he had not ended it by holding up to me, as one example to emulate, a certain fellow student. That particular student stood high in the regard of the staff, but I happened to room near her, and I knew that secretly she broke many institute rules. She also lied about her age to her boyfriends, and so on. I was sure if Dr. Page knew what I knew, he would never have held her up as a pattern of conduct. So I concluded he did not know either of us and brushed the accusation aside. China was later to be a painful revelation to me of my own heart and frailty. From this distance, I now know that Dr. Page had indeed sensed a real flaw in my life, but had hold of the wrong label, that was all.

I was selfish. I had whimsically divided the world into two classes: people who interested me and people who did not. I felt I was not proud, because the people who interested me were often among the poor or the uneducated. My friendship for them was as warm as for those who had social or educational advantages.

Toward people who did not interest me I must have

appeared proud. I cold-shouldered them and brushed them off me as time-wasters. This was of course a serious flaw for a missionary, but I fancy its basis was selfishness rather than pride.

The next point was disobedience. How I did get indignant! There were many rules at Moody Bible Institute which were difficult to keep. The rules have been revised since, and it is no longer so, but I had been meticulous in obeying simply because I had signed a promise to do so. I felt honor bound to keep that promise. The little matter of laundry, for instance. We had washbowls in our rooms, but their use for laundry was forbidden. To rinse one pair of stockings a day was allowed, no more. There was no laundry in Ransom Hall, so I had to waste many weary steps going to another dormitory to do my laundry and waste more precious minutes because I was required each time to get permission from the matron to do so. And I could not always find the matron. This was my most galling trial. The girl who had been held up to me as an example washed all her lingerie and sometimes even nightclothes right in her bedroom at hours when she knew the inspectors would be busy elsewhere, and dried them on her radiator! "The rule is unreasonable" was her only answer when I remarked on it. But I had promised to obey, so I dragged my weary self over to the other building every week. And now the CIM had been told I was disobedient!

I had been told not to spread around this second condition of my acceptance by the mission, but I did write a few friends. They wrote back quickly, indignant and sympathetic, and I was somewhat mollified. All except one. Roy Bancroft was a music student with a beautiful baritone voice and a consecrated heart. We had invited Roy out to St. Charles Reformatory to sing to the boys and help deal with them. I happened to be writing to him those days and impulsively told him. A letter came back quickly, and I opened it with a smile of anticipation, thinking Roy, too, would be indignant on my behalf. I got a shock.

"Isobel," he wrote, "what surprised me most of all was your attitude in this matter. You sound bitter and resentful. Why, if anyone had said to me, 'Roy B., you are proud, disobedient, and a troublemaker,' I would answer: 'Amen, brother! And even then you haven't said the half of it!' What good thing is there in any of us, anyway? We have victory over these things only as we bring them one by one to the cross and ask our Lord to crucify it for us."

These words "stabbed my spirit broad awake." Faithful friend he was, not afraid to season his words with salt even as he did not forget to speak with grace also. I was on my knees in no time asking the Lord to forgive me.

I arose from my knees with a different attitude. Instead of resentment there was alertness to watch and see if these three horrid "diabolutians" — pride, disobedience, rebellion — were there lurking in my camp. The town of "Mansoul" should not protect them if detected. This brought me into peace, even though I always shrank from the memory that I was to be watched for their appearance in my life.

Subsequently I learned in a most unexpected way of my detractor's identity. Then I knew the reason for her hostility. She was a teacher in a school I had attended. She wished me to assist her in spying on my fellow pupils. I felt that was unworthy and so had incurred her displeasure by refusing.

When I learned this, I was tempted to clear myself with Mr. Brownlee and the Western Council. But should I? I seemed to hear a voice say, "If that had been said of me, I'd have answered 'Amen, Brother! And then you haven't told the half of it!'" Dear old Roy! He was right. Why try to make the mission think I was lily white? They'd have personal experience before long as to just how earthly a person I was!

"No, Lord!" I whispered. "I won't bother the mission with it. But how princely of You to let me know. It is like a miracle. Only You could have done it."

For the Lord is always kind
Be not blind.

Kind? To let me end up at Moody, where I had striven so to be faithful, under such a cloud? To let me begin with the CIM under such a stigma? Kind?

Yes. You see, the Lord foreknew there was a work to be done in Vancouver before I sailed for China. If I had ended up institute life with great éclat I would quite possibly have wrecked that work at the very outset. My self-confidence needed to be thoroughly jarred before He dare put this delicate affair into my hands. And He jarred it all right. My Master is thorough, and "no one worketh like Him." But He had also been meticulously kind. Just as soon as He dared, He showed me why. That after-graduation ceremony experience of His enfolding love has blessed me all my life.

Only by searching can we find out what He is.

To jump ahead of my story again, but to complete this little matter, when the door did open for China again, Mr. Thomson wrote me a letter. I cannot quote it verbatim, but it ran like this: "I have never mentioned to you that little condition of the Toronto Council. From the first, both Professor Ellis and I felt there was a mistake somewhere, and I want you to know that so thorough was our confidence in this that I have not felt it even necessary to call the Western Council together. I telephoned each one of them, and we all want you to know that you are accepted by the China Inland Mission unconditionally and unanimously. Every one of them said that. And our loving prayers and blessings go with you."

I bowed my head over that little letter and wept tears of gratitude. Yes, my Master is thorough. He wounds, but He binds up, and His balm of Gilead heals without stinging. It cools, refreshes and restores in every part. He gives the garment of praise for the spirit of heaviness and brings beauty out of our ashes.

CHAPTER TWELVE

THE VANCOUVER GIRLS CORNER CLUB

Father and I traveled on the train together from Toronto to Vancouver where my brother Murray met us at the station. It was strange to be together without Mother. It was still more strange to find myself going across the ferry to North Vancouver in order to get home.

Father and Murray had rented a small four-room bungalow on Twelfth Avenue. Dad had one bedroom, I was given the other, and Murray put up a cot in the sitting room at night and slept there. The fourth room was a kitchen. A bathroom separated the two small bedrooms, and a good big basement took in my trunk and suitcases. The little place was scarcely big enough for the three of us.

There were familiar things in the house — Mother's piano, the well-known parlor chairs, friendly bookcases, and a big fireplace — just like the one in the old home. It was good to be back, and I came to love that little house on the hill. From the front porch I could see the harbor and the waters of Burrard Inlet, beyond which lay — China.

There now faced me the need for employment. I must earn my living until the door to China reopened. Was I to go back to school teaching? I would have to sign a contract and then would not be free to leave if the way opened before the contract expired. I felt great reluctance in spirit to do this. God had led me out of school teaching. I felt it would be like sending Abraham back to Ur of the Chaldees to return to it.

While I was praying and pondering I received an invitation to speak to the Vancouver Girls Corner Club (VGCC) at their evangelistic service on the next Tuesday night. Yes, I replied, I would be very pleased to be their speaker. Then, hanging up the phone, I asked my father who the VGCC were.

"Christian business girls banded together to try to win other business girls to the Lord," Father answered. "The Club was founded by Mrs. Neff, a worker in the big evangelistic campaign held here when you were in your teens. Don't you remember? Well, when the meetings were over they had a final supper with the converts, and some of the business girls got into a corner to discuss how they could keep together and keep going on after the campaign ended. They decided to form a club and to hold a weekly meeting to bring in unsaved friends. "Here we are in a corner," one said jokingly. 'Let's call it the Corner Club.' And that is how it started and how it got its name. It is a fine work, and I am glad you are going to speak to them."

The next Tuesday evening Father took me downtown to the club rooms. They had a big lounge overlooking Granville Street, one of the busiest streets of the city, a small office for their superintendent, and a big dining hall where we went for supper. On Tuesday evenings a good supper was furnished for only fifteen cents a person. The dessert was always cake, and those delicious cakes were baked and donated by the women's societies in various churches, thus enabling the supper price to be kept low.

After supper the tables were cleared, pushed back, and the chairs arranged for the meeting. A platform and piano stood at the end of the long room where a bright evangelistic service was conducted for an hour. Christian business girls themselves led this meeting. It was an enjoyable time, I thought.

In less than a week I received a second phone call. It was from the girls' president of the VGCC. She astounded me with an invitation to become their superintendent! I had not noticed that the position was vacant, but apparently they had been without one for some time. "We feel shy to ask you to take it," the president said, "because we can't afford to pay you the salary you deserve, or even as much as we have paid in the past. Corner Club is run down a bit, having gone so long without a superintendent. We can give you only eighty dollars a month to start with, but as the work picks up we hope to increase it. Your hours will not be heavy, and you will not need to be in the office until ten o'clock each morning.

When I asked what the duties of superintendent were, she replied, "Well, to lead and direct the work. Every day at noon, tea, coffee, and milk are sold in the dining room. Business girls bring their bag lunches there and enjoy getting hot drinks to go with them. You will circulate among these girls, get to know them, and try to lead them to the Lord. Every Tuesday evening you will be in charge of the evangelistic service and will speak. The Corner Club has had to draw speakers from various churches in the city during this period without a superintendent, and we would like to pay back our debt to them, so to speak, by having you speak at any of their young people's societies who invite you. This would also advertise the club.

"And maybe you yourself will create some new activities. Remember, our motto is The Other Girl."

I asked for time to pray about it, and a date was set for my answer.

Nothing else was offered to me, and as I waited in prayer I felt the Lord wanted me to accept this invitation. So it came about that I became superintendent of the Vancouver Girls Corner Club for 1927 and part of 1928. I had stipulated that the moment the door to China opened, I should be free to resign, and that was agreed to.

I now entered upon a fascinating period of my life. Corner Club was run by a Girls' Board, a Women's Board — representatives from different churches and denominations in the city — the superintendent, and a business manager.

The business manager was a godly, middle-aged woman whom everyone called Mother Fitch. Mrs. Fitch was one of those energetic saints who are described as being full of good works. She had not enjoyed a higher education but had been taught of the Spirit. She lived for the glory of God and the winning of souls. There was no big evangelistic effort in Vancouver without Mother Fitch having a hand in it somewhere. The city missions were enriched by her prayers and practical services. Realizing that God had not trained her for platform work, she humbly accepted any mundane service — cooking, serving, or even scrubbing — and prayed it into a ministry of blessing. Every Sunday she went to the jails to preach. During the week she ran the kitchen department of the Corner Club. Needless to say, I found in her a kindred spirit, although she must have been more than twice my age. We were a queer-looking team, but always a united one.

The Girls' Board were elected by members of the club. I was only twenty-five years old by now, and most of the Girls' Board, I think, would have been a bit older than that, but our times together are among my happiest memories. I have always felt that my Corner Club girls were among the loveliest young women that God ever made. They were ready for any venture that would win souls, but they were also a very merry group. The club rooms resounded with laughter and gay banter in between the earnest prayer meetings and discussions.

I did not meet the Women's Board immediately, and Mother Fitch laid hold of me early in that first week with a warning. "Isobel," she said, "I would like to suggest to you that you do away with the Women's Board. They are not spiritually minded like the Girls' Board, and I think they may be a drag on you. I believe God has sent you here for a red-hot soul-winning campaign, and I am behind you one hundred percent. You preach and I will cook! I know my place.

"The Women's Board won't allow you to give a call to decision on Tuesday nights. I'm afraid you will meet with other restrictions. The club does get support from their churches, and they would cut it off if the Women's Board were dissolved. But I am willing to live by faith like Hudson Taylor, and I am sure you are, too. I think you could talk the girls into agreeing; they are anxious to give you a free hand to direct things as God leads you."

This was a delicate situation into which I had come. I was young, inexperienced, and the words red-hot soul-winning campaign thrilled my soul. To give up a salary and live like Hudson Taylor would be heroic — the strongest kind of appeal to me at that time.

It was many years before a quiet article in the CIM's private News Bulletin alerted me to the danger of missionary heroics. The article pointed out that just because a line of action is difficult, painful, or dangerous does not necessarily prove that it is the will of God. A simple illustration was cited: A call for medicine comes in the middle of a missionary's meal. She jumps up and leaves her food half eaten and rushes off to answer. That may seem noble and sacrificial on the surface, but in reality it could be foolish and harmful. Of course, I am not referring to life-and-death emergencies, when promptness is a duty. I mean an ordinary medical call. The messenger has probably dillydallied several times already, and an extra ten minutes' wait until the nurse's needed nourishment is properly masticated will hurt no one.

As I read the article, I recognized my own behavior pattern with deep chagrin. I was not given to breaking up my mealtimes, but I had been guilty of other extremes of conduct. Some natures are more open to this temptation than others, and mine is one. So at this time of my youth, Mother Fitch's suggestion appealed to me as quite possibly the highest line of conduct. I was cautious, however, and told her we must pray much before doing anything so radical.

I believe it was that very evening when I met the president of the Women's Board. She was a warm-hearted Scottish lady who shook hands with me, giving me a hearty welcome to the Corner Club. Then she added: "You are a candidate of the CIM, aren't you? I'm good friends of Mr. and Mrs. Charles Thomson, and he told me to keep an eye on you and let him know how you get on here!" She beamed at me cordially, perfectly unconscious that she had just brought a whiplash down over my shoulders with a sting!

I never for a moment thought that Mr. Thomson had betrayed our secret to her. Charles Thomson was a godly Scotsman, the soul of honor and common sense. I was sure that Mrs. Mc– did not know the full implication of what she had said. But I saw in a second that I was in no position to begin my superintendent's career by dismissing her! Some more gentle method must be found. The Lord used this whiplash to guide me onto a better road.

I told Mrs. Fitch that I felt we should go slowly and try what prayer could do first. She sighed, but never refused a challenge to pray. The day was to come when the president of the Women's Board would kneel beside me in the little office, and with tears thank God that He had brought me to Corner Club. Likewise with tears in my heart, I thanked Him for keeping me from the precipitate action which would have wounded this dear life and hindered the accomplishment of His purposes.

As I gradually met with other members of the Women's Board I found a group of women very different in temperament one from another, but gifted, reasonable, and cooperative. They did ask that I issue no calls to come forward for decision, feeling that the business girls would prefer more decorum and dignity in the Tuesday night services than the usual penitent form method. But they too wanted to see people converted.

God blessed the Tuesday night meetings in a quiet way. Not many made an open profession of Christ (which troubled me) but the attendance grew by leaps and bounds. No one knew how difficult I found those services. I was tormented by a fear of having stage fright again, or of my mind going blank like it had during the MBI graduation ceremony. Many a Tuesday night, as the girls were gaily putting out the hymn books, I slipped down the corridor to the bathroom, the only place where I could be sure I was not seen. Leaning up against the wall, I cried to the Lord for nerve to go back and get on that platform. He never failed me. The stage fright never came back seriously. Gradually I began to count on His help, and speaking grew easier.

Invitations to churches began to come, too. Finding that several of the girls had beautiful voices, I organized and trained a quartet, following the teaching I had received at Bible school in this. One of the younger members of the Women's Board had a bell-like contralto voice suited to sing the bass part, so the quartet represented both the Girls' and Women's Boards and was a real success. "Miss Miller and the Corner Club Quartet" began to get calls from all different denominations, and our opportunities to witness for the Lord multiplied.

Often we took our suppers to the club and ate before leaving as a team for the church of the evening. Then the dining room rang with laughter. All four had a keen sense of humor and the relaxation from their office work prompted an ebullition of youthful spirits. But always, the evening's work was brought before the Lord in earnest petition before we left.

I began to see what a power a Christian business girls' club could be. Through its interdenominational character, it was quietly reaching out and challenging young people's societies in many denominations throughout the city.

Even into the business life of the city an influence was going out. A lawyer asked what had caused the change in his stenographer. Her answer had an effect on him. More and more, I saw the wonderful potential of the work when first things were kept first. There have been corner clubs in other cities, but the temptation is to let them sink into merely social service efforts.

Young life must have an outlet. I soon saw that, so we had picnics, seaside corn roasts, hikes on Saturday afternoon, and in the winter we had a stunt night for girls only. This was one of the most hilarious evenings I ever spent. The stunts were all wholesome fun and revealed much brains and talent. I myself had opened it, dressed up as a cartoon version of an old maid schoolmarm. I announced that the students of my boarding school were about to put on a program for their relatives and friends. Most of the girls had never seen me lay aside the dignity of my office just for fun, and it tickled their fancy to find I could enjoy a joke as much as the next one.

The stunt night broke the ice between me and a certain girl for whom I had been fishing in vain for several weeks. It was only a short time afterward that she accepted the Lord in my office. But all our parties were threaded through with the love of Him and a deadly earnestness that others might find Him too. I think that is the secret. A merely social club helps nobody very much, for it does not offer any solution to the problems of life.

My noontime circulating among the lunchers was to me the most difficult part of my work. Always shy about meeting strangers, I also had this unfortunate background of having so fiercely resented personal work in my own earlier days. It made me timid to barge in on other lives. I always felt I was a failure in those noon contacts where a gifted evangelist could no doubt have reaped a big harvest. But I made friends and had their confidence. The sins and temptations which they gradually opened up to me about were appalling and led us into many unexpected adventures.

Let me tell about two of them.

Edith was a clever young girl who had come out from England to get work in Canada. She lived with an aunt. She met and fell in love with a young man. We followed her joy through the day she appeared in the lunch room with her new diamond ring to the time when she said goodbye to office work and invited us all to her wedding. She had her dress and trousseau, had resigned her job, the wedding day was set, and the invitations had all been mailed. A night or so before the wedding her telephone rang. Edith heard a strange woman's voice on the wire. "Is it true that you are to be married to Mr. So-and-so in a couple of days?" the voice asked.

"Yes," answered Edith, wondering.

"I am very sorry, but I must tell you he is already married. I am his wife. I have our wedding certificate here."

Can you imagine the shock of this to that young English girl? The shame of it? The heartbreak — for she had given her love unreservedly? But you cannot imagine the worst. Her aunt, humiliated at having to cancel the wedding, in a towering rage ordered the girl out of the house. She would have no such thing of shame under her roof, she said.

Out on the streets, homeless, wild with grief and heartache, where could Edith go? Her church? They were her aunt's type and would probably hold the same views. Corner Club. She crept in, broken, distraught, then found herself clasped on Mother Fitch's broad bosom. Corner Club protected her, loved her, found her a home, and led her to the Lord. She proved to be an exceptionally gifted girl, and it was only a year or two before she had earned enough money to go back to England, where her own mother still lived. It was a soul saved and a young life saved as well.

The most exciting story perhaps was that of Flossie. A knock on my office door came one afternoon and I opened it to see a fashionably-dressed woman standing there.

"Miss Miller?" she asked. "May I have a word with you? I have been to your club rooms several times and admire the work you are doing very much. There is a young girl named Flossie in my boardinghouse who needs help. May I tell you about her?"

I led the woman into the lounge and we sat while she talked. "Flossie is a nice young thing from the prairies. Her mother is a widow, I believe, who sent her to Vancouver to study to be a nurse. She is a pretty girl and seems to have a lot of dates with young doctors, you know, and I guess she neglected her studies. Anyway, she failed her year, is out of the hospital, and has no money. I am anxious that the temptations of a big city do not suck her under. Do you think your Corner Club could help her? I told her you were very nice, despite — ahem — your long hair, and — ahem — your long skirts" — this with an eye to each. The fashions in 1927 had shrunk skirts until they barely reached the knees. Although I had shortened my dresses I still felt that modesty required that the knees be covered. My hair should be long for the China of those days, so I had never cut it.

I was much amused at her two "ahems" but boldly ignored this little difference of opinion between us. "We will certainly do anything we can to help Flossie," I answered. "We are not an employment agency, but—"

"But do you have dishes to wash and dry?" urged the lady. "I thought if you could employ her here it would give you a chance to talk to her and perhaps steady her."

"I will consult our business manager," I replied. "Leave me your telephone number and I will call you. We do have dishes to wash, but our help is voluntary. Our budget does not allow for much paid labor."

Mother Fitch, of course, was enthusiastic about taking in another young life to influence for Christ. It was agreed to employ her for a week or so while we sought to get her regular employment. So Flossie was brought to us.

She turned out to be a gay little chatterbox. Most of the time she was busy in the kitchen, of course, but there came an hour when I was able to have her alone in the office. I presented the claims of the Lord Jesus for her heart and life. She listened with the tears running down her face and acquiesced in everything. When she had left, Mother Fitch came in to inquire about the result.

"Well," I answered slowly, "I am not satisfied. She was certainly touched, and willing to follow me in prayer and accept Christ as her Savior. She wept, but somehow I cannot believe she is born again. Something did not seem to click, if you know what I mean."

Although we were not an employment agency, and certainly not a rescue mission, still it was possible at Corner Club to announce to the girls that a certain one needed work and to ask that the members keep their eyes open for a suitable vacancy. This we did, and Flossie was not with us long before a noon-hour girl named Helen came to my office.

"Do you suppose, Isobel," she said, "that this girl Flossie would be willing to take a poorly paid job until something better turns up? My mother has had a stroke and is completely paralyzed. She can't even turn in bed. I am only an office worker and can't afford a trained nurse to care for her during the day while I am away. But Flossie has had some training. I would give her room and board and a little pocket money if she would come and care for Mother."

We called Flossie in and she accepted the position. She would be free every evening and we urged her to come to our Tuesday supper and service, and said goodbye. As our lives were full of unexpected cases, it was not possible to follow up Flossie very closely.

Summer came and I was to have two weeks' vacation. I chose to spend it at The Firs. A few days before I was to leave, I had a telephone call from Helen.

"Isobel, have you heard about Flossie?" she asked.

"No, not a word," I said in alarm. "Please tell me."

"Well, she is in the hospital. She began to act and talk strangely here, and one evening she had a sort of spell. So I called in a doctor. He sent her to her old hospital and now says she is insane. I don't believe it myself. In fact, I think she is acting a part to get away from here. It is a bit quiet for her, I guess. I feel she's been accustomed to hit the pace, you know. Anyway, I wish you would go and see her. Her doctor might believe you. He won't listen to me. Here is his name and telephone number.

I was staggered at this news, but promised to go and see Flossie. Helen hung up and I called the doctor's number. A crisp, professional voice answered.

"Doctor, this is Miss Miller, superintendent of the Vancouver Girls Corner Club. I believe you are treating Flossie –?"

"Yes," he said, shortly.

"Well, our club is interested in her, and I have been asked to go and see her at the hospital if you will allow it."

"It would do no good, Miss Miller," came the answer quickly. "She would not know you. She recognizes no one, and I have had her put in the violent ward."

"Well, Doctor, the friends with whom she was staying feel that she is just acting a part."

An exclamation of anger stopped me. "Miss Miller, I have been a specialist in mental cases for many years. Do you presume to tell me I cannot recognize insanity?" He was clearly insulted.

"No, Doctor. I beg your pardon. But for the sake of her friends, could you not give me permission to visit Flossie? My pronouncement would quiet them."

He gave an exclamation of impatience. "All right. Be at the hospital on Saturday afternoon at two. I'll give orders for you to be admitted." He slammed down the receiver.

Down went my phone, too. And up went my heart

to the Lord. "Now, O Lord, I'm in for it! I have a new search on now. Can you control the high-strung bunch of nerves which is me and enable me to face an insane person?"

I think most people must have a private horror, a phobia, about some one thing. Most women fear snakes. I've known a big man almost to go to pieces at the news that a rat was near. A famous scholar of our generation admits to a phobia regarding insects. My own private fear has always been insanity. I don't like snakes or rats, but they do not set my nerves a-jingle like the word insane.

"Lord," I prayed, "when I felt I should go down into that cellar to see if Mrs. Mac had hung herself there, I asked You for the nerve to go, and I didn't get it. Of course, You knew she wasn't there and that I didn't need to look. But still, can You nerve me to face insanity? Saturday afternoon will be my proving time."

I was to leave on Saturday night for The Firs, so I was packed and ready for the train. Leaving my baggage at the Corner Club, I proceeded to the hospital at two o'clock in the afternoon and inquired for the ward where Flossie was. It was in the basement. Across the corridor were heavy, locked doors, and in front of them, at the side, was a desk with two nurses in attendance. On the other side of the doors, someone was singing a ragtime song at the top of her lungs.

I went up to the nurses and said, "Please, may I see Flossie –?"

The nurses looked at one another. "I'm sorry," said the elder of the two. "It's against the rules. No one is allowed to see her."

"But I was told that I might, if I came at this hour," I said.

Again they exchanged glances, then the younger nurse said to me, "She is violent. That is her singing now." The youthful voice was rollicking on.

"The doctor told me he would give orders to let me in," I protested. That was a magic word. "Oh," they said, scrambling through some papers on the desk. "Yes, here is an order for a Miss Miller."

"I am Miss Miller."

"All right. Step this way."

The nurse took a big bunch of keys and opened the corridor door, ushering me into the aisle on the other side. Small cells lined this corridor on both sides, and each door was locked. The cells were beneath ground level, but had one iron-barred window high up near the ceiling level with the ground outside.

My heart was beating so violently I felt dizzy and sick, but before I knew what was going to happen, the nurse had unlocked a cell and pushed me in alone. I heard her lock the door behind me!

Flossie stood with her back to the door, looking up through the little barred window and shouting her song. She was in a disheveled mess that would not be a kindness to describe. At the sound of the key in the door she whirled around like a wild animal about to spring on its prey, but as soon as she saw me she went limp. She blinked stupidly for a moment, then said, "Miss Miller!"

"Yes, Flossie dear," I answered. Going forward and taking her in my arms, I kissed her. "I've only just learned that you were sick. I've come to see you. Get into bed, dear, and then we can talk."

Like a lamb she climbed on to her cot. I sat at the foot of it as there was no chair in the cell, nothing but the iron bed. I talked about the Corner Club, trying to draw her memory back to quiet things and to the Lord. She answered each question intelligently and only once did she exhibit anything strange. I was telling her of some little Corner Club incident and said, "Mother

Fitch — you remember who she is, Flossie, don't you?"

"Yes," came from the young face on the pillow. Then there followed an expression of cunning. "And I know you," she cried emphatically.

I went cold all down my spine, but ignored it, continuing my quiet chitchat. I told her to trust in the Lord and promised to write her mother. "I am going on my vacation," I said, "but will come and see you as soon as I get back."

I stayed about fifteen minutes, then knocked loudly on the door, hoping the nurse would hear. She came at length, and I left, leaving Flossie still lying quietly in bed.

When I got back to the Corner Club I telephoned the doctor. "Yes," he said. "Well, how did you get on?"

"She knew me immediately, Doctor, and called me by name."

There was a staggered silence at the other end of the line. Then I heard him say to himself, "Well I'll be —." To me he said, "Miss Miller, please tell me exactly what happened, right from the first." After I had done so, he said, "How soon can you visit her again?"

"I am leaving in a few hours for vacation, Doctor. I will be gone two weeks, but will call you as soon as I return."

"You do that!" he said earnestly, and we hung up.

I felt that Helen must be right. Flossie was playing a part for some reason. If I had known it was so important, I would have given up my vacation to attend her, but I didn't. In my next telephone conversation with the doctor on my return from The Firs he told me she had been sent to an insane asylum outside Vancouver. He was quite indifferent whether I visited her or not. "This time she won't know you," he said, but he gave me permission for a visit with her.

Looking back at this incident after nearly thirty

years, and after having had more than two decades of experience with devil-worshiping mountain tribes, I am inclined to think Flossie was demon possessed. The devil has hoodwinked educated America into thinking he is a myth, and he is working havoc unrecognized. My reason for believing this is twofold. First, I found that the mere presence of a consecrated Christian in a demon-haunted house was enough to force back those powers. My entrance into that hospital cell brought with it the power of my Master and the demon force was temporarily quelled. Second, that look of cunning when she affirmed — unasked! — that she knew me, was the very same that I have seen on the face of a demon-possessed tribal girl just before that demon was cast out. And the compulsion to confess recognition is similar to what took place in our Lord's day. But as superintendent of the Corner Club, I knew as yet nothing of these matters.

Now I felt I must visit Flossie in the asylum. Again I was terrified at the thought, but as God had taken care of me in the hospital, He would surely help me in this second step. So one afternoon found me arriving by bus at the famous institution which I had never dreamed I would ever see.

It was a huge place several stories high. As I approached the large entrance, men patients behind the iron bars of a veranda screamed out to me and thrust their arms through the bars as if trying to reach me. Not very soothing to the nerves! Inside, I was ushered first into the office of the resident physician. He was a young man, and as I advanced to his desk he exclaimed, "Why, it is Miss Miller!" It was my turn to be astonished.

"Isobel Miller of Arts 22, UBC (University of British Columbia), isn't it?" he repeated, shaking hands cordially.

"Why, yes. But how do you know?" I queried.

He laughed. "I was an undergraduate, a year or so behind you. What have you been doing since then?"

We had a little chat. My work at the Corner Club brought up the name of Flossie. There must have been several thousand patients in that place, so I asked, "Would you possibly know Flossie?"

"Would I?" he returned. "I'll never forget the night they brought her here. It took four strong men to hold her!"

"What do you think? Is she incurable?"

"No-o," he answered thoughtfully. "This type is brought on by dissipation and with the use of modern drugs we can often effect a cure. Did she talk very much? That is the first sign of this condition coming on — extreme talkativeness. She'll be here two years at least, though, and then there is likely to be a recurrence later on."

"My club would like to help. Of course, we believe that prayer will help her, but is there anything else you can suggest?"

"Yes," he answered. "She is run down through late hours and the life she led. If your club can send her nourishing food, with extra protein values, such as meats and broths, that might hasten her recovery. The ordinary food here is good, but she needs extra meat and such, which a government institution can hardly provide."

I promised we would do our best, and he rang for an orderly to show me the way to Flossie's ward.

"They must prepare her to see you," he warned, "so you will have to wait awhile."

Again I was taken to a corridor with a locked door. A lounge opened off at the side where harmless patients were sitting around, some embroidering, some reading, one playing the piano. A nurse at a desk was obviously in charge. I sat on a bench opposite the locked door.

Up tripped a young woman who asked me boldly, "Who have you come to see?"

"Flossie–," I replied with uncertainty.

"Oh yes, a nice girl, I know her!" This with a loud voice, her eyes on the matron at the desk. Then behind her hand in a whisper she said to me, "She is no more insane than I am."

"I've brought her some chocolates. Do you think she'll like them?"I asked, more to make conversation than anything else.

"Oh, yes. The food here is fine!" This also in a loud voice toward the matron, then behind her hand in a whisper, "It's awful. They starve us. Bring her lots of chocolates!" And so she went on — compliments in a loud voice for the matron to hear, and complaints in a whisper behind her hand to me. It was all I could do to keep my face straight, but evidently she was known to them. After a few minutes the matron quietly lifted her head and ordered, "K–, you come back in here."

"See our bondage!" whispered the woman, making a wry face to me. But she obeyed.

At length a nurse came with a key, and I was again ushered in behind the door to where a second nurse had brought Flossie. Then to my horror, both nurses left me alone and locked me in with the patient.

I would not have recognized Flossie. She was so thin, a mere shadow of herself! The preparation they had given her was to drug her into stupidity, then immerse her, hair and all, in a bath to clean her up. She stood before me swaying unsteadily, her damp hair clinging to her like a drowned rat. She obviously did not know me. I told her my name and repeated it, but she gave no sign of recognition. I proffered the chocolates, and she opened them eagerly, popping them into her mouth one after the other rapaciously. Within five minutes I knew that conversation was useless. It was true, she did not know me nor could she follow my thoughts.

Then the effect of the drug began to wear off. She had been brought to me in a corridor, with rooms on both sides. "I want to go back!" she said suddenly and started staggering down the corridor, hunting for her own room. As I did not know which one it was, I knocked and banged on the locked door to call the nurses back. But by this time Flossie had evidently come to. She turned fiercely on the nurse, swore, and cursed her. A glimpse into the room showed me why they had to drug her and bathe her before allowing any other human being to see her. Obviously she was living like an animal.

Heartsick, I turned away and came home. It was an experience I would not care to have often, but the Lord had strengthened me to go through with it.

At the Corner Club I did not describe what I had seen, but merely gave the doctor's advice to send her nourishing foods. I told how emaciated she was and asked for prayer. I also wrote to her mother and the result was that a sister was sent to Vancouver to visit Flossie and care for her needs.

Prayer was made constantly for the poor child's recovery. The girls and the Women's Board sent cartons of jellied chicken, homemade broths, jellies, and other good foods. Still we were not prepared for our dear Lord's answer to our prayers, abundantly above all that we had asked or thought.

Within six months Flossie was dismissed, cured. After asking the Lord daily to do this, I was taken aback by the speed with which His answer came. One day I received a telephone call from a stranger which ran something like this: "Miss Miller, you do not know me, but I am Mrs.–, neighbor of Flossie's mother on the prairies. My husband and I are on a trip to the coast, and Flossie's mother asked me to bring Flossie home with me when we return. Do you know she was dismissed from the hospital a few days ago? No? Well, she was. She is living with her sister, but would like to come and see you before she leaves and thank you for what you have done for her. May I bring her this afternoon? We leave by the evening train. Thank you. At three o'clock then."

I sat back in my swivel chair and gasped. Then I bowed my head and thanked the Lord.

I awaited three o'clock with a little trepidation. I had met two very different Flossies already. Which would this one resemble? The gay chatterbox? The doped animal? Could she really be normal?

The third Flossie was the real Flossie and a distinctly different person still. She had gained weight to a pleasing plumpness, but was so shy and quiet I could hardly recognize her. She thanked me prettily and sincerely, but when she had gone into the kitchen to salute Mother Fitch I turned to their neighbor and said, "My, she is quiet! Do you think she is afraid of me?"

The lady widened her eyes with astonishment. "On, no. Flossie never did talk much. She was always the quiet one. She is just like she used to be. Her mother will be delighted."

And so we parted. But my story isn't ended.

Nine years passed. I was back at the Corner Club as a missionary on furlough, a married woman and a mother. What a welcome they gave me! Before the first message, which they asked me to give at the old Tuesday evening hour, I had a telephone call. "Isobel, I wonder if you will remember me. This is Flossie."

I nearly jumped out of my skin. "Flossie! You back in Vancouver?"

"Yes. But I'm married now. Oh, Isobel, the Lord has been so good to me. I want to tell you all about it before you meet my husband. Will you take supper with me downtown, just the two of us alone? Then I will go with you to the meeting. My husband is coming to the meeting tonight. I got permission to bring him, since John, another man, will also be present. But I want you to hear my story first."

I wonder if you can understand my joy. No one can who has not mothered spiritual children. No one can who has not stood and watched the brand blazing in the fire, and then shrunk from the heat which almost scorched the hand stretched out to snatch it from burning!

That evening in a little cubbyhole of a restaurant we sat face to face once more. She was still sweet-faced Flossie, her quiet manner lit up with heartfelt gratitude. "Yes, I have a good husband and two darling children. And I've never had a recurrence. I'm sure the Lord won't let me now. And Isobel, I want my children to be brought up in the church. My husband and I are agreed: we want a Christian home."

Just one little peach from a year's harvest at the Corner Club. What potential lies in such work — leading business girls to Christ!

Often, on furloughs, I have heard the impatient remark, "Why go to the foreign field? There is lots to be done at home here!" There most certainly is. And there are lots of Christians at home. But are they doing it?

By searching for Him He makes us conscious of the need of others and helps us cut channels by which He may be poured into their lives. In no time we find ourselves His fellow workers, and life is rich.

But I must come back to my tale, for by now the door to China was opening again.

CHAPTER THIRTEEN
"LET US GO ON!"

It was the spring of 1928 when the China Director of the China Inland Mission, the Rev. George Gibb, paid a visit to Vancouver. I was called in to meet him and well remember the searching look of concern he gave me. "My dear girl," he said, "you look worn out. Are you well enough to go to China?"

"Oh, yes. Physically I am sound. But I am very tired," I admitted. Our home on the north side was so far from the evening church appointments. Late at night, the ferry did not run so frequently, and if I missed one there was a long wait before the next. Often it was midnight before I got to bed, and six o'clock was my rising hour if I was to have a quiet time, get the house chores done, and catch the nine o'clock ferry.

But I think most of it was emotional fatigue. Mentally I knew the way of victory. I had read of Hudson Taylor's experience, *The Exchanged Life*, when he rolled all his burdens on the Lord. I had heard Keswick teaching expounded at The Firs and had seen it lived in lives there. But how to transmute it into experience was beyond me. I secretly worried about things. My father's Micawber-like attitude toward business appalled me. Where would he end up? Now I knew what my mother's secret trial had been and how much we all owed to her sound judgment and carefulness.

I worried about my own failure at the Corner Club. I did not have the gift of evangelism. Young lives were constantly being cleansed, rededicated and built up in Him, but I did not see that. I looked just for souls to take the initial step of salvation. Pentecostal girls were urging me to seek the baptism of the Spirit. One of them was a gifted evangelist, a gold-haired, angel-faced girl, and I fell into the snare of comparing myself with others. Peggy had something I didn't. Was it really the speaking in tongues? Inwardly I fretted. But the Lord was carefully holding me. I asked Peggy and Dorothy, another girl who kept at me, to describe what happened when they were "filled with the Spirit." Their most vivid descriptions were no more than what I myself had often experienced when alone with the Lord and the awareness of His presence would flood in. I had never spoken in tongues, but I seemed to have had everything else they claimed to have experienced. This kept me from going off into doctrinal extremes.

I always felt there was a peril in seeking just an experience from the Lord. The temptation is to think the experience has sanctified. It hasn't. These uplifting times in His presence, provings of His faithful care, enrich us, add to our joy. But they do not sanctify us. They do not make us stronger Christians. They do not make us holier than our fellows, as I was to learn to my shame. But they do make us richer in our knowledge of Him, and they give us joy that addeth no sorrow to it.

The only way to be holy is daily to hand over to the Holy Spirit what Dr. Tozer calls "the hyphenated sins of the human spirit . . . self-righteousness, self-pity, self-confidence, self-admiration, self-love, and a host of others like them . . . which can be removed only in spiritual experience, never by mere instruction. As well try to instruct leprosy out of our system. There must be a work of God in destruction before we are free. We must invite the cross to do its deadly work within us. We must bring our self sins to the cross for judgment." The Holy Spirit will crucify these things for us as we hand them over to Him. We must accept the suffering involved, rejoicing in the knowledge that His resurrection life will be the final outcome.

So, with all my rich experience of answered prayers, I was still full of worry, self-pity, and many other ugly things, but I was not acutely conscious they were there.

Mr. Gibb was really perturbed. By now I wore an engagement ring, and John Kuhn was already in China and being used of the Lord there. If my health broke, would that bring John home? Mr. Gibb consulted Mr. Thomson, and they both ordered me to resign from the Corner Club and take six months of complete rest before sailing in October, 1928. Mr. Gibb intended to give instructions that I be put on mission support in order to do this, but, most unusual for him, he must have forgotten. I waited and waited, but the mission sent me nothing. I felt I should not petition them for it. Hudson Taylor would have just prayed.

I forget how it happened, but Mr. and Mrs. Whipple heard of the order for me to rest and invited me to spend the five or six months at The Firs. I could help in cleaning cabins and getting the conference grounds ready, but first I was to have a full month of nothing but rest — even breakfast in bed!

I had been able to save no money, for I had felt I should pay my father's debts. It was clear to me that the next invention would never bring him an income, and I was right. So I landed at The Firs with about thirty-six dollars — all the money I had left.

No one can know what it meant to me to be taken in by dear cheery Mrs. Whipple, and be given the upstairs porch which they were fixing up as bedroom for their own daughter, Lois, when she should return from the

Bible Institute of Los Angeles, where she was studying. Two sides of the room were without full walls and the scented, tall fir trees were its screen. Mrs. Whipple had procured some old cement sacks. These she had bleached, stenciling a pretty fleur-de-lis pattern on them, and hung them up in lieu of walls. When the opening of the conference would bring many people around and the fir trees might not afford privacy enough, these curtains could be drawn. But when I arrived, the scented green needles were the wall, and I loved it. To wake up in the morning having slept to the full, no pressure of schedule upon me, to hear the birds caroling and the sun trying to peep at me through the green foliage was like living with God in Eden. I can never forget it.

I knew the Whipples were "living by faith," but had no idea that when they took me in that first night they were down to rock bottom financially. I felt I would like to give them my thirty-six dollars. Before going to bed, I handed the money to her, saying, "I want you to take this. It won't pay for all I'll eat these months, but I'd feel happier if I felt I'd given something."

I remember Mrs. Whipple flushed a bit and tried to refuse, but I insisted. Then the matter left my mind. She told me years afterward that it was one of the hardest things she ever did, to take my money. But the milk bill was due in the morning, and she had nothing else with which to meet it. And I would need milk. My money fed us until a gift of sixty dollars came in, and from then on there was no shortage. This is just a glimpse of how the Whipples lived: although the gifts had been few, they did not hesitate to invite me to live with them for six months. And I do not need to say how God blessed them.

They had returned from China to find that The Firs was the only home they had. With funds low and the need to make and furnish a bedroom for Lois — and me! — they were put on their mettle. From the attic of a relative they obtained some old furniture, free. This, they sandpapered and repainted a pretty green for Lois's bedroom. When the stenciled curtains were hung, it was as dainty a room as a girl could wish — and I had learned lots about how to convert old things into new!

The conference that summer (1928) was the most blessed I had ever known. The special speaker was Dr. Arthur Harris of Wales, and the Spirit of the Lord was powerfully among us. For one thing, Mrs. Whipple had prayed that every young person attending the conference would yield to the Lord before going home. One evening during the service she was impelled to go to the girls' dormitory. There, she knelt by each bed, claiming for Christ the occupant of that bed. Needless to say, every evening there were decisions made.

Toward the last evening there were a few who still hung back from full surrender, so the staff called us leaders of the young people to pray all during the evening service. I can never forget that prayer service. The Spirit of the Lord came down upon us as in apostolic times, and we all started to pray simultaneously out loud. I was not even conscious of the others. I was so lifted up into the Lord's presence and so burdened for the souls that were hanging back that it was not until a break came that I suddenly came down to earth and realized that we had all been praying aloud together. From the upper room where we prayed, down through the treetops, we could see the open-air auditorium. As we prayed, one after another of the recalcitrant ones got up and went forward in surrender. The very last, a girl for whom I had held little hope, has now been for decades a most faithful missionary on a foreign field. Very truly it was the work of the Spirit of God.

Conference over, I needed to go back to Vancouver and get my outfit ready for China. There were still no funds sent to me by the mission, but a love gift from my brother paid my fare home. (When Murray saw Dad's invention was not likely to make him rich, he had set about getting a job.) But where would the next money come from? To add to the perplexity came a letter from Marjorie Harrison saying she was traveling in our parts and would like to stop off and see us. When I answered with a cordial invitation, I did not have enough money to pay her carfare from the station to our home, let alone feed her.

Then I got a call from Mr. Thomson to come to his office. There was some money waiting for me.

At last! I said jubilantly to myself. Mr. Gibb had remembered his promise! But it was no such thing. It was much more wonderful than that. It was fifty dollars from my own dear John in China! I think it was the remainder of a bank account he had left over from his earnings in preparation for Bible school days. "I want to have a share in your outfit," he wrote, "but it has no strings on it; you may use it for any need."

The first bit fed Marjorie!

From then on I had no difficulty. The Corner Club girls gave me showers and a beautiful outfit, which included the money to buy a portable organ. That little organ went with us to the Salween mountains and brought much joy to the Lisu as well as to us missionaries for many years.

I prayed much about my final message at the Corner Club. I did not know, though I shrewdly suspected it, that some of those dear girls were going to prove prayer warriors for whom I would thank the Lord all my missionary days. It has been so now for twenty-eight years. God laid on my heart a message for myself as well as for them from Hebrews 6:1, *Let us go on*.

The search is not ended. We have only begun to explore our eternal, unfathomable God. "Let us leave behind the elementary teaching about Christ and go forward to adult understanding. Let us not lay over and over again the foundation truths . . . No, if God allows, *let us go on*," paraphrases Phillips. And that was the burden of my message.

On October 11, 1928, I sailed for China. There was quite a large party of us, one being the little American girl who roomed next to me in Ransom Hall at Moody Bible Institute. Ella Dieken was engaged to Jack Graham, and we were to be roommates at the language school in China.

My father had permission to sail with me on our steamer as far as Victoria, so the emotion of parting from him did not take place at the wharf in Vancouver. The ship was due to pull out about noon, and the Corner Club girls forsook their lunch and flocked down to the wharf. They made such a crowd that a stranger asked my brother, "Who is the girl who is getting this send-off?"

"Just an unknown missionary going out for the first time" was certainly not the answer expected. But God can give special things to His unknown children when He wants to.

At last a bugler climbed up to the highest bridge of the *Empress of Russia* and began to play Queen Liliuokalani's beautiful farewell song, *Aloha Oe*. It is, of course, the sad parting of two lovers. It breathes passion, but no certitude of hope. It is earth doing its best to reach out for cheer, but failing mournfully. I am so glad that Christian words have been set to that music for such moments. Only Christians dare to say, "We never part for the last time." As the bugle notes poured forth on the noisy air of the wharf, there gradually grew a stillness over the crowd.

In these the closing days of time
    What peace this glorious thought affords
That soon, O wondrous truth sublime,
    He shall come, King of kings and Lord of lords

He's coming soon. He's coming soon
    With joy we'll welcome His returning
It may be morn, it may be night or noon
    But oh, He's coming soon.

But "the gospel must first be published among all nations" (Mark 13:10).

And we, who living yet remain
    Caught up shall meet our faithful Lord.
This hope we cherish not in vain
    But we comfort one another with this word.

The last notes quavered sadly on the high air. The unbelieving in the crowd, grasping the only best they knew, whispered, "Aloha Oe." The big anchors rattled as they pulled up, the paper streamers began to tear as the mighty ship slowly drew away from the wharf. Beloved girl faces were working with emotion, and one or two were crying. "Lord," I whispered, "give me a last word they won't forget." A thrown voice could still reach the wharf. I leaned over the side and called out slowly, "Let us go on!"

The light of heaven broke through the tears of earth on some faces, so I knew they had heard. They waved their hands in a signal of assent and the *Empress of Russia* turned her stately head slowly toward the Narrows, Puget Sound, the Pacific Ocean, and — China.

But there was one more step. At the city of Victoria, on Vancouver Island, my father said goodbye and disembarked. After he had left, the purser brought me a telegram. It read simply, WE WILL GO ON —YOUR CORNER CLUB GIRLS.

Tears of gratitude rained in my heart. Twenty-eight years have passed — a good, long testing period. The Corner Club is still operating. Most of those girls have gone on with the Lord. There are people in more than one country of the world who rise up and call some of them blessed. One of them on the wharf that day had unconsciously been leaning on me rather than on the Lord Himself, so she sprawled spiritually when her human prop was removed. But on the whole they kept their promise.

Now, as reader and author part, I can find no better words to use than these same, "Let us go on." Go on searching and exploring the greatness and the dearness of our God.

He has no favorites. He has said, "Ye shall find me when ye shall search for me with all your heart" (Jer. 29:13).

Notice that last phrase, for it is the only condition. There must be inner honesty and undivided loyalty — that is the only stipulation. "The man who trusts God, but with inward reservations, is like a wave of the sea, carried forward by the wind one moment and driven back the next. That sort of man cannot hope to receive anything from God, and the life of a man of divided loyalty will reveal instability at every turn" (Jas. 1:6-8 Phillips).

But — "He is a rewarder of them that diligently seek him" (Heb. 11:6).

Said Susanna Wesley, "He is so infinitely blessed that every perception of His blissful presence imparts a gladness to the heart. Every degree of approach to Him is, in the same proportion, a degree of happiness."

So — *let us go on* — SEARCHING.

BOOKS BY ISOBEL KUHN

Ascent to the Tribes

By Searching

Children of the Hills
(formerly titled *Precious Things of the Lasting Hills*)

Green Leaf in Drought

In the Arena

Nests Above the Abyss

Second-Mile People

Stones of Fire

Whom God Has Joined